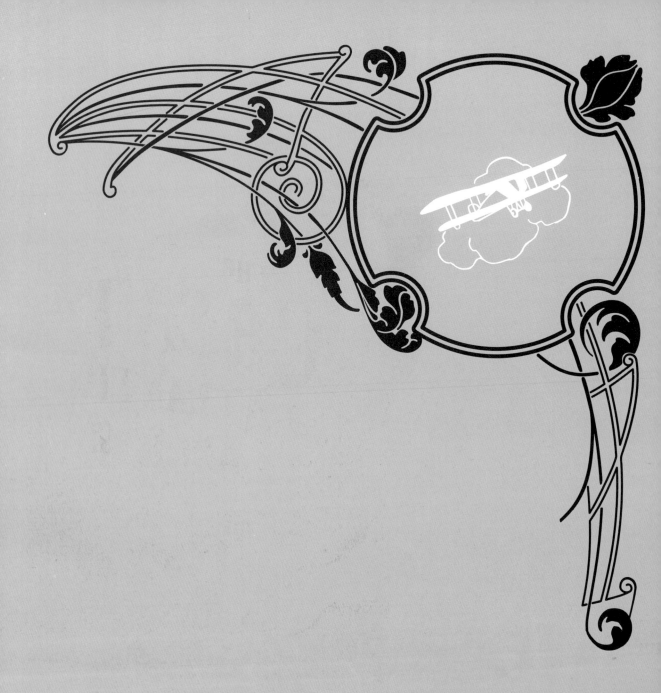

THE GREAT ATLANTIC AIR RACE

Gavin Will owns *Boulder Publications*, a book publishing firm in Newfoundland, Canada, that specializes in non-fiction. Previously, he worked as a business journalist, writing for *Reuters*, *Bloomberg News*, the *Globe and Mail*, and several oil industry publications. With a lifelong love for history, his interest in transatlantic aviation was piqued by the central role Newfoundland played during the pioneer years of aviation, when such well known pilots as Amelia Earhart and Charles Lindbergh visited its shores during the 1920s and 1930s.

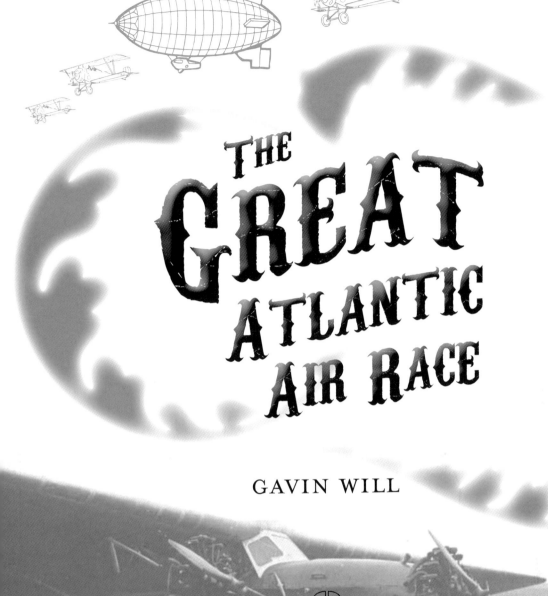

THE GREAT ATLANTIC AIR RACE

GAVIN WILL

THE O'BRIEN PRESS
DUBLIN

First published 2009 (as *The Big Hop*) by
Boulder Publications,
Portugal Cove-St Philip's,
Newfoundland and Labrador,
Canada.

This revised and updated edition
first published 2011 by
The O'Brien Press Ltd.,
12 Terenure Road East,
Dublin 6,
Ireland.
Tel: +353 I 4923333;
Fax: +353 I 4922777
E-mail: books@obrien.ie
Website: www.obrien.ie

ISBN: 978-1-84717-231-0
Text © copyright Gavin Will 2008

I 2 3 4 5 6 7 8 9 IO
II I2 I3 I4 I5 I6

Cover graphic courtesy of iStockphoto.
Cover photograph courtesy of Queen Elizabeth II Library, Memorial University.
Printed and bound in Malaysia.

Editor's Note
This edition contains revised text, maps and new material.
World rights, excluding Canada, reside with The O'Brien Press.

CONTENTS

AUTHOR'S NOTE

This book was inspired by Robert Tait, who wrote an unpublished manuscript on the exploits of aviators who used Newfoundland as their departure point for reaching Europe after the First World War. Tait, a war veteran who became Newfoundland's diplomatic representative in Boston, was among the throngs who gathered in the city of St John's — the easternmost point of North America — to watch as mechanics and pilots prepared their aircraft for journeys across the ocean. Among the historic flights he witnessed was the first successful Atlantic crossing, by John Alcock and Arthur Whitten Brown, to Clifden, Ireland, in 1919.

Today, in an era where passengers travel in temperature-controlled jumbo jets that cruise serenely over continents and oceans, it is difficult to appreciate the dangers that early aviators faced as they strove for glory. By 1919, powered flight was barely beyond its infancy; the Wright brothers had flown their first rickety plane in 1903, only sixteen years earlier. Significant improvements in aircraft performance soon followed, particularly during the First World War when they were used for reconnaissance and "dogfights" with enemy planes. Bombers, which made an appearance by the end of the war, were converted for long-range travel after the conflict ended; several of them were used in transatlantic attempts in 1919.

Despite steady improvements in technology, prior to the mid-1930s flying was hazardous — particularly in inclement weather — and aircraft engines were prone to failure. Reliable aerial navigational techniques were primitive, and radios even worse. But early aviators knowingly risked their lives to cross the world's oceans because the rewards were tantalising: prize money was offered by newspapers and wealthy patrons, tickertape parades were attended by hundreds of thousands of people in New York, and audiences with European royalty were virtually guaranteed.

Pilots shared the public spotlight with movie stars; continental air races, endurance flights, daredevil antics, altitude records, and ocean crossings fed an insatiable public interest. Newspapers, magazines, radio stations, and cinematic newsreels provided blanket coverage of pilots and their feats during the 1920s and 1930s.

But the public was not content to watch its heroes from afar – people yearned for the day when they themselves would be able to fly, although without the dangers faced by early transatlantic aviators. Crossing oceans by air was particularly enticing, because planes offered a much quicker alternative to passenger ships.

Until the mid-1930s, passenger flights across the Atlantic were conducted by airships, most notably the *Graf Zeppelin* and the ill-fated *Hindenburg*. But the future lay with fixed-wing passenger planes, and by the mid-1930s several large airline companies and aircraft manufacturers had emerged that were capable of developing reliable, cost-efficient aircraft.

The pioneering era of aviation ended with the onset of the Second World War. Technological advancements made during the ensuing conflict, combined with the proliferation of modern airports with paved runways, made passenger flights safe and convenient.

This book chronicles those early years of transatlantic flight, with particular attention paid to the men and women who made possible the world of aviation we recognise today.

SIKORSKY AMPHIBIAN

DORNIER "DO X"

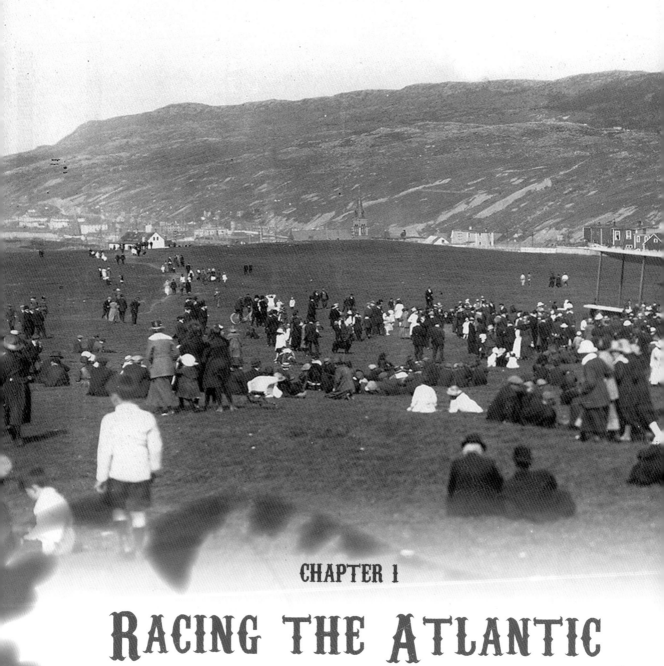

CHAPTER 1
RACING THE ATLANTIC

n February 1919, a passenger liner glided through the narrow water-way that cuts between the grey austere cliffs guarding the entrance to St John's, the capital city of the island of Newfoundland.

The voyage from England to North America's easternmost outpost had been difficult for those on board the ship, and not just because of the notoriously stormy weather encountered in the mid-Atlantic: passengers and crew had faced an outbreak of influenza, a disease that was proving as deadly as the bullets that had killed millions of men during the four years of conflict that had ended just three months earlier.

Pages 8–11: The £10,000 prize offered by Britain's Daily Mail *to the first non-stop transatlantic flight provided a much-needed diversion from the horrors of the First World War. In 1919, four crews travelled by ship to Newfoundland from England; one arrived in Harbour Grace while the others established camps in the city of St John's. Among them was the team of John Alcock and Arthur Witten Brown (main photograph previous pp8–9), who assembled their plane at Quidi Vidi Lake after one of their competitors, the* Raymor, *crashed during takeoff from there. The Cochrane Hotel in St John's became a temporary home to the aircrews. This page inset left: (from left) Kenneth Mackenzie-Grieve, Frederick Raynham, Harry Hawker, and Charles Morgan. Navigator MacKenzie-Grieve and Australian pilot Hawker formed the crew of the Sopwith* Atlantic. *Pilot Raynham with Morgan as navigator manned the rival former bomber,* The Raymor *(seen right and below).*

Among those who contracted influenza during the voyage was Charles Morgan, a veteran British aviator now working for the Martinsyde aircraft manufacturing company, based in Surrey, England. Morgan, who had recovered by the time the ship reached port, immediately began searching for an open field suitable for launching an aircraft across the vast expanse of the Atlantic Ocean.

Morgan's hunt for a makeshift airfield in St John's started a whirlwind of speculation, since his activities marked the first tangible evidence that an air race across the Atlantic was set to begin.

● ●

Opposite left: Close-up view of the nose of Hawker and Mackenzie-Grieve's Sopwith aircraft, after being recovered by USS Lake Charlotteville. *The wreckage and a mail bag were salvaged and taken to Falmouth, England. Below: Hawker and MacKenzie-Grieve's Sopwith* Atlantic *aircraft before its fated flight. Below right: Harry Hawker (far right) and Kenneth Mackenzie-Grieve became the first airmen to attempt a non-stop transatlantic flight. They took off from Newfoundland on May 1, 1919, but engine trouble forced them to ditch the aircraft into the ocean. Following their rescue, the* Daily Mail *awarded them a consolation prize of £5,000.*

● ●

The focus for this competition was provided by Lord Northcliffe, owner of Britain's *Daily Mail* newspaper, who in 1913 offered a prize of £10,000 (US $50,000) to the first aircraft to fly between Europe and North America.

Because of the outbreak of war, no serious plans to claim the prize were made prior to 1918. By the latter stage of the conflict, however, dramatic improvements

had been made to aircraft range and reliability, due largely to the development of bombers capable of reaching cities and factories deep inside enemy territory.

In 1919, as companies and airmen from several countries publicly mulled over their intentions to compete for the prize, Northcliffe altered the rules to favour British flyers. Competitors from former enemy nations were now banned outright, a non-stop stipulation was added, and claimants had to land in either Great Britain or Ireland.

The non-stop amendment was made to exclude the United States Navy, which was planning to fly specially designed Navy Curtiss flying boats to the Azores from Newfoundland and then continue on to Lisbon and England.

With the rules thus altered, Britain's largest aircraft manufacturers assembled teams of flyers and mechanics. As an advance man for the Martinsyde team, Morgan spent several frustrating days in St John's tramping through snowdrifts in search of sufficient flat land to launch an aircraft. He wrote:

I had the pick of what there was, but after spending days going all over the place and plodding through the snow with a kind of alpenstock [staff], the best I could find was a field beside Quidi Vidi Lake just outside St John's. I caught influenza on the way over, which depressed me, and the disappointment over the aerodrome turned me really gloomy.

Morgan may have harboured misgivings about his pending adventure, but residents of St John's were eagerly anticipating the competition. Few Newfoundlanders, aside from soldiers returning from Europe, had ever seen an aircraft, and there is no record of anybody from this small, independent nation flying as either a pilot or a passenger prior to 1919.

But now, even as people mourned the carnage wrought by the First World War, excitement was building as Newfoundland prepared to host the greatest air race the world had ever witnessed. Having found an airstrip for Martinsyde, Morgan went back to England, but he returned to St John's in mid-April with pilot Frederick Raynham and a biplane, a former bomber christened *Raymor*.

By then, St John's was already hosting another British team, this one sponsored by the London-based Sopwith Aviation Company, which was led by pilot Harry Hawker and navigator Kenneth Mackenzie-Grieve. With the Quidi Vidi Lake site in St John's already taken, the Sopwith crew sought another airstrip for their biplane, and settled on Glendenning's farm in what is now the city of Mount Pearl, adjacent St John's. After several weeks spent reassembling and testing their aircraft, the Martinsyde and Sopwith teams came to a gentleman's agreement whereby the first team ready to take off for Europe would alert the other prior to their departure.

Not only were the British teams in a race with each another, they were facing competition from the US Navy. Although their flying boats were ineligible to claim the *Daily Mail* prize because of a planned stop in the Azores, the Americans were intent on winning a partial victory over their British competitors. In its bid to cross the Atlantic the navy ordered four custom-built flying boats from Curtiss Aeroplane and Motor Company, then the dominant aircraft manufacturer in the US. Dubbed NCs, or "Nancies", three of the planes took part in the expedition, while the fourth was used for spare parts.

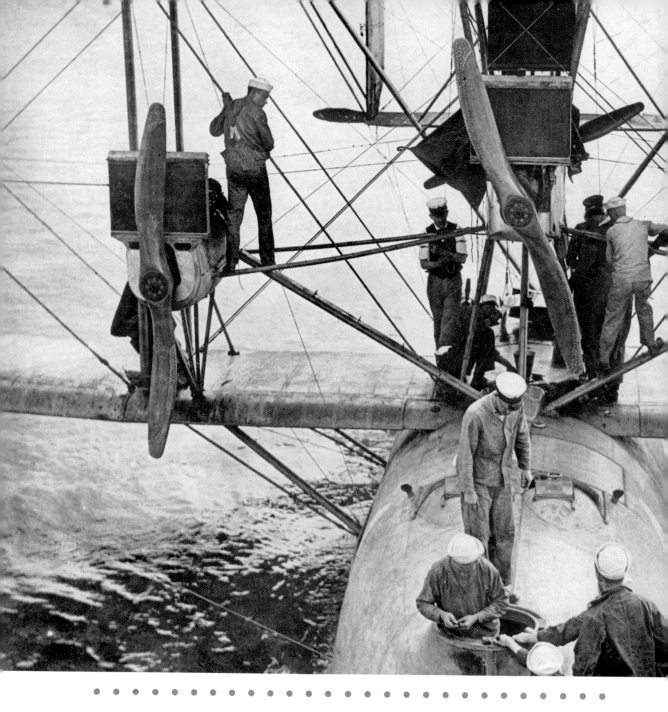

The NC-1 (p15), was one of three United States Navy flying boats to make a transatlantic attempt in May 1919. The isolated Newfoundland community of Trepassey was selected as the launching point because of its sheltered harbour. The NC-4 (above) was the only one to reach the Azores intact. It then flew to Portugal and Great Britain.

On May 10, two of the flying boats, the NC-1 and the NC-3, flew to the Newfoundland community of Trepassey. A few days later they were followed by the NC-4. Located 150 kilometres from St John's at the virtually treeless southeastern tip of the Avalon Peninsula, Trepassey became a temporary naval base, with ships anchored offshore in a support role for the aircraft.

The *Daily Mail* contestants had no direct support from the British military. However, the Trepassey-based flying boats were supported by the full might of the US fleet, with forty-one navy ships positioned along the route to the Azores to serve as beacons to the aircraft. The Americans, led by Commander Richard Byrd, intended to win bragging rights for achieving the first non-stop flight across the ocean, even if the country did not have a plane capable of travelling that far without stopping to refuel.

Without Byrd's leadership and persistence, it is doubtful if the US would have been as keen to embark upon this ambitious transatlantic venture. Byrd, who joined the navy in order to become a pilot, had hoped to take part in combat during the First World War. To his disappointment an incurable leg injury kept him out of any combat role, and he resigned in frustration from the navy in 1916. Byrd remained active as a reservist, however, and when the US joined the war in 1917 he again hoped to fly a plane across the Atlantic and join American forces fighting in Europe.

Instead, in mid-1918 Byrd was appointed to establish a US Navy station in the east coast Canadian province of Nova Scotia, at Baker's Point on the outskirts of the harbour city of Halifax. Baker's Point, which is now part of Canadian Forces Base Shearwater, became home to several flying boats, airships, and kite-balloons, which were used to guard Allied ships from German U-boats. A second American surveillance base was established at North Sydney, another community in Nova Scotia, located on Cape Breton Island. A third base, which was planned for Cape

Broyle, a community situated halfway between St John's and Trepassey, was cancelled when the war ended in November 1918.

With peace, the navy focused on Byrd's transatlantic project, using its new NC flying boats. Byrd had hoped to fly one of the aircraft across the Atlantic, but again his ambitions were dashed, this time by an edict issued by his superiors that the planes be crewed entirely by men who had not participated in a combat zone. The rationale for this rule remains obscure, but it applied to Byrd.

The navy did allow Byrd to command the American transatlantic effort, however, which included one more dramatic element besides the flying boats. On May 15, 1919, spectators dashed to the shores of Quidi Vidi Lake and watched in awe as a blue cigar-shaped airship sailed serenely over St John's. The US Navy planned to fly the C-5 blimp non-stop to Europe from Newfoundland. Under the command of Emory Coil, it had flown from Montauk Point, Long Island, and, after arriving in St John's, was now tethered to the ground close to the Martinsyde biplane.

The C-5 was awaiting the arrival of Byrd, who was travelling by train to St John's from Trepassey to meet the airship, before Coil and his men set off across the ocean. But the crew underestimated the ferocity of maritime storms in Newfoundland, and high winds suddenly tore the C-5 from its moorings on the day of its arrival in St John's. Two crewmen leaped to the ground – one of them sustaining serious injuries – before the airship was carried out to sea. It was never seen again.

• •

Right: The C-5 blimp, seen here shortly after it arrived in St John's in May 1919. High winds tore the blimp from its moorings and carried it out to sea. The C-5 was one of a series of lighter-than-air craft designed by the US Navy following the First World War. The crew of six men flew 1,650 kilometres from Long Island to Newfoundland in 25 hours and 50 minutes, on the first leg of a planned transatlantic journey.

• •

Although the airship was out of the contest, the Americans still had their flying boats, which were now ready to attempt an ocean crossing. With the two British air teams bogged down in testing their machines, many of the dozens of reporters covering the air race boarded a train to visit the windswept, barren landscape of Trepassey. They would not be disappointed, for on May 16 they watched as the three flying boats took off and headed southeast for the Azores. The journey would prove to be a perilous one, even with support from the US fleet. Each flying boat carried a radio, but all three instruments proved unreliable. As a result, the crews had to rely heavily upon visual beacons provided by the naval vessels which were strategically lined up along the route to the Azores.

However, a dense fog bank soon rendered this assistance useless and the three aircraft flew blind for much of the journey. The NC-1, under Lieutenant Commander Peter Bellinger, encountered engine trouble and landed at sea 320 kilometres from the Azores. A ship rescued the crew, but the plane sank. The NC-3, piloted by Commander John Towers, became lost in the fog and also landed on the ocean, 120 kilometres

short of the Azores. Rough seas damaged the NC-3 to such an extent that it could not take off again, but Towers and his crew were able to guide the craft by sea to Ponta Delgado in the Azores using the plane's engines and propellers.

Only the NC-4, under the leadership of Lieutenant Commander Albert Read, succeeded in flying to the town of Horta in the Azores. Poor weather and mechanical problems delayed its departure to the Portuguese mainland until May 27. The NC-4 landed in Lisbon after a ten-hour flight and reached its final destination, Plymouth, England, on May 31.

The departure of the flying boats from Trepassey accelerated Hawker and Mackenzie-Grieve into action, and they hastily decided to attempt their flight to Ireland before the Americans succeeded in reaching Lisbon. On May 18, the Sopwith plane, named *Atlantic*, took off and began its 3,000-kilometre flight to Ireland. The plane's undercarriage, which had been intentionally dropped into the ocean near the Newfoundland coast, was salvaged and later placed on display in a museum.

. . . .

The presence of a four-engine Berlin bomber in the community of Harbour Grace generated considerable excitement. Admiral Kerr and his crew thrilled people across eastern Newfoundland by taking the massive aircraft on test flights throughout the region.

. . . .

The Sopwith team's departure panicked the Martinsyde crew, and within two hours Raynham and Morgan took off in an attempt at catching and overtaking the *Atlantic*. The *Raymor*, was heavily weighed down by fuel, however, and upon takeoff it rose only six metres into the air before crashing nose-first into the ground. Morgan, who had already endured hardships from this adventure, suffered severe lacerations to his face. Raynham later made a second attempt, using a different navigator, but the *Raymor* crashed once again. With this failure, Martinsyde ordered its crew to pack up the wrecked plane and return to Britain.

Martinsyde were afforded this second, unsuccessful, chance because Hawker and Mackenzie-Grieve had failed to arrive in Ireland. After several days of hearing nothing from the *Atlantic* both men were given up for dead and memorial ceremonies were planned in their honour in England. Fortunately, the services were hastily cancelled one week later when a Danish cargo ship, the *Mary*, arrived in Thurso, Scotland, with Hawker and Mackenzie-Grieve on board. The *Mary*, which did not carry a radio, had rescued the aviators 1,800 kilometres east of Newfoundland. Hawker explained to newspaper reporters afterwards that the engine began overheating soon after takeoff, causing its radiator to boil over. The plane zigzagged for nearly three hours over the main shipping lanes before sighting the Danish ship. Hawker and Mackenzie-Grieve brought their aircraft down at sea, and they were rescued. Hawker said:

> We only wanted a few gallons of water, and there was the whole damned Atlantic underneath us. That's what made me puke — knowing that we had enough petrol to reach Ireland and not being able to do it because of the water.

Lord Northcliffe gave Hawker and Mackenzie-Grieve a £5,000 consolation prize, but the title for making the first non-stop transatlantic flight remained unclaimed. The failure of both the Sopwith and Martinsyde planes then gave a pair of latecomers an opportunity to claim the title. On May 26, a team from the London-based Vickers aircraft firm arrived in St John's. Meanwhile, 100 kilometres west of the city in the town of Harbour Grace, a group sponsored by the Handley Page aircraft manufacturing company and led by British naval officer

Admiral Mark Kerr began assembling a massive biplane.

Finding a makeshift airfield in St John's proved difficult for the Vickers' crew because Martinsyde and Sopwith had already leased the best available land. An agreement was eventually reached to use a farm on the city's outskirts near Mundy Pond called Lester's Field. Eventually, Martinsyde relented and gave permission for Vickers to uncrate and rebuild their modified Vimy bomber at Quidi Vidi, and on June 9 the plane was flown to nearby Lester's Field.

During this time, Vickers' chief test pilot John Alcock and navigator Arthur Whitten Brown, whose parents were American, prepared themselves for the perilous journey ahead. The two men shared similar experiences during the war: they had both been shot down and then served the duration of the war as prisoners, Alcock in Turkey and Brown in Germany.

While Alcock and Brown finished their preparations, Harbour Grace buzzed with anticipation as test flights of the four-engine Handley Page V/1500 Berlin bomber, the largest aircraft built by the Allied forces during the war, began. The Vickers Vimy and Handley Page bombers were similar in that they had been built and tested in the latter months of the conflict, and neither aircraft was sent into action prior to the armistice.

Kerr and his crew of three flew the huge biplane over St John's in early June, thereby adding an element of urgency to the Vickers team. However, persistent problems with the engine's cooling system forced Kerr to delay his transatlantic bid. This gave Alcock and Brown sufficient time to complete preparations of their aircraft, which like the Sopwith plane was also named *Atlantic*. It carried a radio as well as a second fuel tank that was stowed away in the plane's bomb compartment.

As the weather warmed, a festive atmosphere pervaded St John's in anticipation of the Vimy flight. The huge white biplane drew hundreds of people, first to Quidi Vidi Lake and then to Mundy Pond — families brought picnic baskets and small children ran excitedly around the aircraft.

Poor weather over the Atlantic Ocean kept the Vimy grounded for several days, but on June 14 conditions were judged safe, and, in the mid-afternoon, Alcock and Brown climbed into the open cockpit and took off for Ireland.

Good fortune accompanied them for the first hour as the weather remained clear. Their luck soon changed, however, when the small propeller driving the wind-driven electrical generator that supplied power to the radio snapped off. They were now completely alone with no contact to the outside world.

John Alcock (left) and Arthur Whitten Brown took off from St John's (above) on June 14, 1919; they made history by achieving the first non-stop flight across the Atlantic Ocean.

Weather conditions then turned against them as they passed through dense clouds and fog. Unlike pilots of today who use electronic navigational aids, early aviators had to rely upon the sun and stars to guide their planes over the open ocean. With no radio and unable to see anything outside his plane a pilot would be flying blind.

During the night the Vimy entered dense cloud and Brown could no longer navigate the plane. He and Alcock suddenly had no idea which way was up, or whether they were flying parallel with the ocean. When the pitch of the engines began increasing in volume, they suddenly realised that their plane was plunging towards the Atlantic but had no idea which way to turn. Brown recalled:

Apart from the changing levels marked by the aneroid [an air pressure gauge], only the fact that our bodies were pressed tightly against the seats indicated that we were falling.

When the plane finally broke through the cloud cover, it was only forty metres above the ocean. Alcock managed to gain control just in time to avoid plunging into the waves. Brown said they could hear the ocean "as its waves swelled, broke, and swelled again."

The temperature fell below freezing as the night wore on, causing ice to form on the plane's wings, fuselage, and controls. Icing increased the difficulty of steering the plane, and the additional weight meant that fuel consumption rose. The men, completely exposed to the elements in an open cockpit, also suffered from the cold.

With daybreak, Alcock brought the Vimy down to warmer air near the ocean surface in order to melt the ice. The engines stuttered from ice that remained lodged in the air intakes, but fortunately they did not cut out altogether.

At 8:15 a.m. the men were relieved to finally catch sight of the coast of Ireland. Their ordeal was over and they knew they had achieved what no one had done before. After sixteen hours and twenty-seven minutes in the air, Alcock landed the plane on what appeared to be solid ground. It turned out to be a bog (the bog of Derrygimlagh Moor near Clifden in County Galway). The wheels of the aircraft sank and its nose plunged into the soft ground. Fortunately, neither man suffered any injury.

• •

British Cabinet Minister Winston Churchill (above left) presenting John Alcock and Arthur Whitten Brown with a cheque for the Daily Mail prize of £10,000. The airmen were greeted by large crowds in England after their aircraft crash-landed in Ireland (left). After a harrowing overnight flight, lasting sixteen hours and twenty-seven minutes, John Alcock guided the biplane onto what he thought was a grassy field at Clifden, Ireland. It turned out to be the bog of Derrygimlagh Moor, however, and the aircraft tipped nose-first into the ground.

• •

MAKING HISTORY AT 120 MILES AN HOUR.

ATLANTIC FLIGHT ACCOMPLISHED.

"I'M ALCOCK—JUST COME FROM NEWFOUNDLAND!"

TWO THOUSAND MILES IN SIXTEEN HOURS:

THRILLING TALE OF STRUGGLE AGAINST CLOUD BANKS, FOG AND SLEET.

CLIFDEN'S AND GALWAY'S FAME.

CONQUERING MAN-BIRDS HONOURED IN THE CITY.

"DAILY MAIL" PRIZE WON.

Full Record of the Greatest Flight in History.

"I'm Alcock—just come from Newfoundland." In this cryptic sentence Capt. Alcock, D.S.C., announced to the awe-stricken Marconi operators on Sunday morning that he and Lieut. Arthur Whitten Brown had just arrived from another hemisphere.

The £10,000 prize that had been awaiting some conquering man-bird more daring—and more fortunate—than the rest since April 1, 1913, had been won. The old world and the new had been bridged in flight. The miracle of other waves that sent the voice of man over vast spaces from hemisphere to hemisphere had been superseded. Man himself had come on the wings of the wind. The Atlantic had been flown at the second attempt in a single night. That touching meeting in Derrygimla Bog on Sunday morning, June 15, 1919, marked a new era in history and made County Galway for ever famous.

When Alcock introduced himself to the wondering wireless men, he uttered an epic in six words, and changed, as with a breath, the current of history and romance.

Irish journalist, Tom 'Cork' Kenny, gained a scoop when he was the first journalist on at the Alcock and Brown crash site. His article appeared in the Connacht Tribune.

Today the historic flight is commemorated locally by a cairn four kilometres south of Clifden where Marconi had his first transatlantic wireless station, and a sculpture of a tail-fin on Errislannan Hill just north of the landing spot. Alcock and Brown's Vickers Vimy biplane can be seen in the London science museum.

After being treated to a reception in Dublin, Alcock and Brown travelled to Britain by ship, arriving at Holyhead in Wales. Their heroics were rewarded with a triumphant procession through London, followed by the presentation of their £10,000 award by Winston Churchill, then Secretary of War. In addition to receiving the *Daily Mail* prize, Alcock and Brown were both knighted by King George V.

With Alcock and Brown's victory, Kerr abandoned his transatlantic quest Instead, he and his crew accepted an invitation to fly to New York and tour the United States with the Handley Page machine. They flew to the town of Parrsboro in Nova Scotia on July 4, but a heavy landing on a makeshift airstrip destroyed the plane's fuselage. The aircraft was repaired, and it reached New York in October. It was soon damaged again while making a forced landing at Cleveland, en route to Chicago from New York. At this point the tour was cancelled and Kerr returned to England.

Despite their triumph, both Alcock and Brown suffered misfortune in the months and years that followed.

Alcock died six months later on December 18, 1919, when, while flying a plane from England to an air show in Paris, he crashed in northern France.

Brown only flew across the ocean one more time – to New York in 1946, to celebrate the commencement of commercial passenger flights between North America and Europe. His son Arthur, who flew with the Royal Air Force during the Second World War, had been killed during the D-Day invasion of France in 1944. Brown descended into a depression and never recovered from this loss; he committed suicide in 1948.

Just weeks after the success of Alcock and Brown, while the world was gripped by flying fever, British airmen achieved another transatlantic milestone by making the first round-trip voyage in an airship. The R-34 airship measured 196 metres, twice the length of a football field, and was known as 'Tiny'. Built at Inchinnan, near Glasgow in Scotland, during the waning months of the First World War, the R-34 took off from East Fortune, Scotland, on July 2, 1919, on a round trip to New York. A crew of thirty men, under the command of Royal Air Force officer Major George Herbert Scott, guided the hydrogen-filled airship across the ocean to Hazelhurst Field in Mineola, Long Island.

On board, several modifications were made to the R-34 in preparation for the journey since it was not built as a passenger carrier. This included arranging extra accommodation by slinging hammocks in the keel walkway, and hot food

• •

Built at Inchinnan, near Glasgow in Scotland, the R-34 airship completed the first return flight across the Atlantic Ocean in July 1919. A replica can be seen in Mineola, Long Island.

• •

THE GREAT ATLANTIC AIR RACE

was provided by cooking on a plate that was welded to the engine exhaust pipe.

While Scott and his crew became heroes for their exploits, the public's imagination was truly piqued by the stories of two unofficial passengers who went along for the ride. One of them, twenty-two-year-old William Ballantyne from Newcastle, became the world's first aerial stowaway. Ballantyne had worked on building the airship and hoped to be included as a crewman; when this failed to transpire he hid away in the rigging and only emerged after the airship had left on its journey when he became ill from the hydrogen fumes. The second stowaway was a cat named Wopsie, who was spirited aboard by one of the crewmen. Both Ballantyne and the cat became the centre of media attention in the US once the R-34 arrived.

The most dangerous part of the journey came at the midway point of the North Atlantic, en route to Newfoundland, when the airship met stiff headwinds. As it neared the Newfoundland coast, the R-34 was almost pushed back to sea by a series of violent storms.

On July 4, Scott spotted a group of small islands lying off the east coast of Newfoundland. Brigadier General EM Maitland described the sighting of the islands as "the most thrilling moment of our voyage – successfully accomplished the first stage … the first to bridge the gulf from east to west by way of the air." The R-34 had reached Newfoundland at Trinity Bay. A short time later, crossing Fortune Bay, the crew dropped a package of letters to a group of spectators.

On July 6, after four and a half days of flying and with virtually no fuel remaining, the massive airship reached Long Island, delighting the large crowd that watched in awe as it glided to a halt over Hazelhurst Field. Spectators were further thrilled by the spectacle of Major John Pritchard leaping from the passenger gondola with a mooring rope in hand and parachuting to the ground from an elevation of 600 metres.

After only three days in New Jersey, the R-34 began its return flight to England, and reached Pulham in just over three days. In doing so, the R-34 had made the first return crossing of the Atlantic Ocean.

Airships became popular with wealthy travellers during the 1920s and 1930s. Many lives were lost in accidents, however, and the perils of lighter-than-air flight would eventually force passenger airships from the skies. Among those who died in accidents were several R-34 pioneers, including John Pritchard in 1921 and George Scott in 1930.

After the excitement of 1919, many people may have expected similar transat-

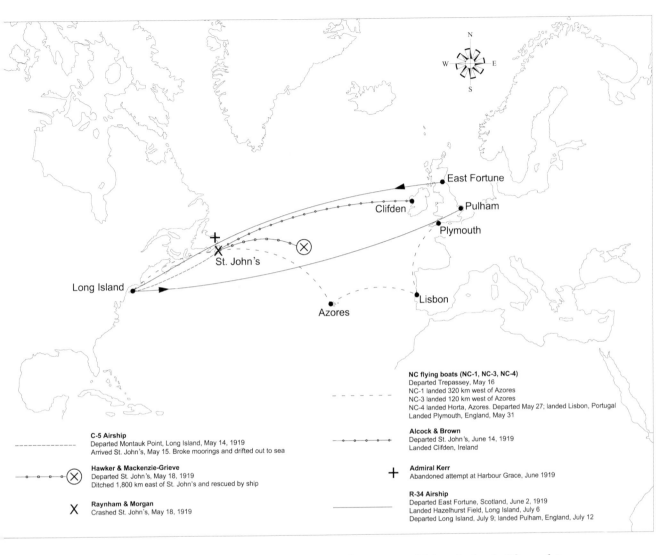

C-5 Airship
Departed Montauk Point, Long Island, May 14, 1919
Arrived St. John's, May 15. Broke moorings and drifted out to sea

Hawker & Mackenzie-Grieve
Departed St. John's, May 18, 1919
Ditched 1,800 km east of St. John's and rescued by ship

Raynham & Morgan
Crashed St. John's, May 18, 1919

NC flying boats (NC-1, NC-3, NC-4)
Departed Trepassey, May 16
NC-1 landed 320 km west of Azores
NC-3 landed 120 km west of Azores
NC-4 landed Horta, Azores. Departed May 27; landed Lisbon, Portugal
Landed Plymouth, England, May 31

Alcock & Brown
Departed St. John's, June 14, 1919
Landed Clifden, Ireland

Admiral Kerr
Abandoned attempt at Harbour Grace, June 1919

R-34 Airship
Departed East Fortune, Scotland, June 2, 1919
Landed Hazelhurst Field, Long Island, July 6
Departed Long Island, July 9; landed Pulham, England, July 12

lantic heroics the following year. But those hopes would be dashed. If anything had been proven from the post-war competition between the US and Britain, it was that aircraft and navigation technology were too unreliable for long-distance flights over the treacherous North Atlantic.

Five years would pass before anyone attempted another ocean crossing. When it did occur, few people would be there to see history being made, for the landing site was on the austere coast of Labrador, a region of eastern Canada frequented by icebergs and Arctic pack ice.

On this barren coast the sound of aircraft engines was heard for the first time in history on August 31, 1924, as a pair of American biplanes flew low over a scattering of icebergs and landed in the uninhabited harbour of Ice Tickle. A group of newspaper reporters watching from the deck of a naval ship, *USS Richmond*, were witnessing the final stages of the first successful flight around the world.

Five months earlier, four seaplanes had taken off from Seattle, Washington, on this ambitious undertaking. The United States Army Air Service (precursor of the US Air Force) organised and financed this round-the-world flight, just as the navy had in 1919 with the flying boats that crossed the Atlantic. The newly-formed California-based Douglas Aircraft Company was commissioned to design and build five planes for the venture, four of which were destined to fly around the world, while the fifth was used for training and spare parts.

In order to improve its chances of its planes flying around the world, the Air Service received support from American military bases and diplomatic offices located along the route. These outposts were used to provide support services to the aircraft and their crews, including repairs, accommodations, and refuelling.

On March 31, the World Cruisers, which were named *Chicago*, *New Orleans*, *Seattle*, and *Boston*, took off from a lake near the west coast city of Seattle, Washington. The contingent was soon reduced to three aircraft when the *Seattle* crashed in Alaska. The crew survived, but the aircraft was demolished.

Governments throughout the world welcomed the three surviving World Cruisers, with the exception of the Soviet Union, which denied requests to allow them into its airspace. The planes were damaged numerous times, but logistical support from American bases and embassies allowed them to keep going.

As the planes reached northern Europe it seemed as if all three would arrive triumphantly in the United States, but bad luck would claim one of the aircraft. In mid-August, while it was flying between the Faroe and Orkney islands, the *Boston* encountered engine trouble and made an emergency landing at sea. A US Navy destroyer rescued the crew, but the *Boston* sank during a botched salvage attempt.

This left only the *Chicago* and the *New Orleans* to complete the world flight. The planes left Iceland on August 21 and arrived in Greenland the same day. Poor weather delayed their departure from the village of Ivigtut. On August 31, the weather cleared and the planes took off. They landed at Ice Tickle in Labrador following a 900-kilometre flight that took seven hours to complete.

Senior US Navy officers greeted Lieutenant Lowell Smith, commander of the *Chicago*, as he stepped ashore. "So that was it. We were in America," Smith recalled.

"A launch came out from the Richmond and took us ashore after we had moved. We had landed after our travel, like Pilgrim Fathers on a large rock, but I'm afraid our first activities were not as edifying as theirs. We were just too darned happy for words."

The two aircraft departed Labrador on September 2, landing after a short flight at Hawkes Bay on Newfoundland's nearby Northern Peninsula. They travelled south over the Gulf of St Lawrence to arrive at Pictou, Nova Scotia, the next day. Here, they were joined by the only World Cruiser not taking part in the expedition – the prototype, dubbed *Boston II*. In Pictou, the airmen were treated to a reception by the local chamber of commerce that included bagpipers and a lobster dinner. Later that day they were invited aboard the Canadian destroyer, *Patriot*, and fed lobster once again.

After leaving Nova Scotia, enthusiastic crowds then greeted the planes as they flew what amounted to a victory tour across the United States. On September 28, the 42,000-kilometre journey ended where it had begun six months earlier, near Seattle.

• •

Below: Crew members of the Navy escort ship USS Lawrence *place a marker on Ice Tickle Island, Labrador, on August 31, 1924 where the aircraft first touched the Western Hemisphere after crossing the Atlantic Ocean Two US Navy planes achieved the first round-the-world flight.*

• •

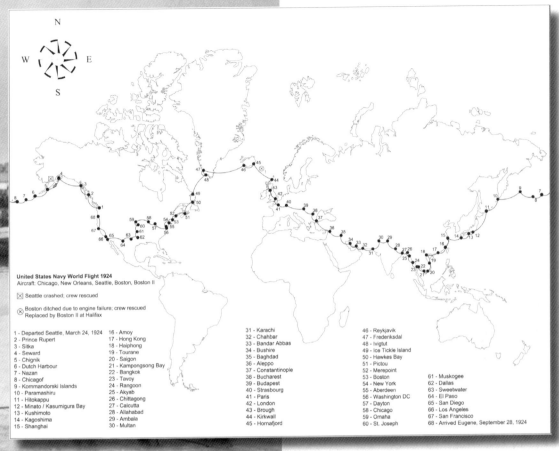

United States Navy World Flight 1924
Aircraft: Chicago, New Orleans, Seattle, Boston, Boston II

☒ Seattle crashed; crew rescued

⊗ Boston ditched due to engine failure; crew rescued
Replaced by Boston II at Halifax

1 - Departed Seattle, March 24, 1924	16 - Amoy	31 - Karachi	46 - Reykjavik
2 - Prince Rupert	17 - Hong Kong	32 - Chahbar	47 - Frederiksdal
3 - Sitka	18 - Haiphong	33 - Bandar Abbas	48 - Ivigtut
4 - Seward	19 - Tourane	34 - Bushire	49 - Ice Tickle Island
5 - Chignik	20 - Saigon	35 - Baghdad	50 - Hawkes Bay
6 - Dutch Harbour	21 - Kampongsong Bay	36 - Aleppo	51 - Pictou
7 - Nazan	22 - Bangkok	37 - Constantinople	52 - Merepoint
8 - Chicagof	23 - Tavoy	38 - Bucharest	53 - Boston
9 - Kommandorski Islands	24 - Rangoon	39 - Budapest	54 - New York
10 - Paramishiru	25 - Akyab	40 - Strasbourg	55 - Aberdeen
11 - Hitokappu	26 - Chittagong	41 - Paris	56 - Washington DC
12 - Minato / Kasumigura Bay	27 - Calcutta	42 - London	57 - Dayton
13 - Kushimoto	28 - Allahabad	43 - Brough	58 - Chicago
14 - Kagoshima	29 - Ambala	44 - Kirkwall	59 - Omaha
15 - Shanghai	30 - Multan	45 - Hornafjord	60 - St. Joseph
			61 - Muskogee
			62 - Dallas
			63 - Sweetwater
			64 - El Paso
			65 - San Diego
			66 - Los Angeles
			67 - San Francisco
			68 - Arrived Eugene, September 28, 1924

Left: Spectators watch as the New Orleans
is launched into Reykjavik harbour in Iceland
during the round-the-world voyage of the
Douglas World Cruisers in 1924.

While Charles Lindbergh made history by flying non-stop from New York to Paris in 1927, others that year were less fortunate. Mounting fatalities among transatlantic aviators convinced the crew of the Royal Windsor (seen here in Harbour Grace, Newfoundland) to abandon their attempt.

CHAPTER 2
TRIUMPH AND DISASTER

The glory of flying across the Atlantic Ocean tempted many aviators into the sky in 1927 — a year of triumph for a few, but one of disaster for many others.

Once again fame and prize money proved attractive lures, just as they had in 1919 when Alcock and Brown won the competition to cross the ocean by air. A few months after their Vickers Vimy crash-landed in Ireland, French hotelier Raymond Orteig offered US $25,000 to the winner of the first non-stop flight between Paris and New York.

At the time, aviation technology was too unreliable for such a lengthy journey, so nobody attempted to claim the prize until 1926, when French First World War flying ace René Fonck and three crewmen prepared to fly to Paris from Roosevelt Field, the renamed US Army's Hazelhurst Field on

Long Island. The term "field" was apt, as runways in this era were composed of clay and sand because paved surfaces were considered too hard for landing gear to absorb the shock of touching down.

Fonck and his crew planned to fly over Cape Breton, Nova Scotia, and Bonavista Bay, Newfoundland, before attempting to cross the treacherous waters of the North Atlantic. Tragically for them, part of the landing gear collapsed as their Sikorsky S-35 amphibious aircraft gained speed during takeoff. The plane, heavily laden with fuel, plunged over a bank at the end of the airstrip, and caught fire during takeoff. Fonck and navigator Lawrence Curtin survived, but two crewmen died.

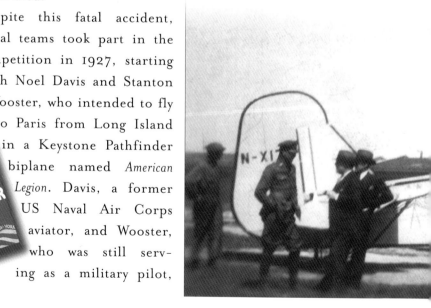

Despite this fatal accident, several teams took part in the competition in 1927, starting with Noel Davis and Stanton Wooster, who intended to fly to Paris from Long Island in a Keystone Pathfinder biplane named *American Legion*. Davis, a former US Naval Air Corps aviator, and Wooster, who was still serving as a military pilot, obtained permission from the US Army Air Services to use a Pathfinder for the transatlantic journey. The two men, who had financial backing from the American Legion, tested the plane at an Army base in Virginia before embarking on their flight to Paris. The amount of fuel necessary to operate the plane's three motors had worried the pilots, however, since the machine weighed 7,700

kilograms when fully loaded. Despite this concern, on April 26 Davis and Wooster took the *American Legion* on its final test flight prior to attempting the transatlantic crossing. As the fuel-laden plane lumbered into the air, its pilots struggled with the controls to gain altitude. Instead of climbing, however, the aircraft lost speed as it cleared a grove of trees. Within seconds it careened earthward, diving nose-first into a shallow pond, instantly killing Davis and Wooster.

• •

In France, Charles Nungesser and François Coli (opposite) were celebrated in song, but the brave airmen disappeared over the North Atlantic. Ships and aircraft along the eastern seaboard, including a St John's–based plane (above), searched in vain for the aviators. They were not the first to die in attempting a New York–Paris flight: two men perished when the American Legion *(below) crashed, and two more were incinerated after their Sikorsky aircraft burst into flames during a test flight in Virginia.*

• •

This accident left three groups vying for the Orteig Prize, and a fourth — led by Richard Byrd — which was competing but did not officially register (and was therefore not eligible) for the prize.

By early May, all four teams were testing their planes and training the men who hoped to make aviation history. On Long Island, three American planes were being outfitted. At Roosevelt Field, Byrd's crewmen were frantically repairing their Fokker aircraft, named *America*, which had crashed during a test flight in April, injuring Byrd and pilot Floyd Bennett. At Curtiss Field, an airstrip adjacent Roosevelt Field, the *Columbia*, a plane owned by millionaire Charles Levine and designed by aircraft builder Giuseppe Bellanca, stood ready. Last to join the fray was Charles Lindbergh, an airmail pilot, who hoped to fly solo to Paris in the *Spirit of St Louis* and had rented a hanger adjacent Levine's at Curtiss Field.

Meanwhile, at Le Bourget Airport in Paris, public pressure was being exerted upon two French First World War veterans, pilot Charles Nungesser and navigator François Coli, to take to the air ahead of the American-led teams. Such fierce competition focused public attention and enthusiasm on the New York-Paris race, and newspapers on both continents were agog with speculation as to who would win the honour.

This frenzy of national pride induced some airmen to take unnecessary risks during the early years of aviation; and in the race for the Orteig Prize, the French aviators may have allowed patriotism to take precedence over safety. The westward route planned by Nungesser and Coli, with Paris as their departure point, appealed to French public opinion, but the hazards were greater than an eastward crossing, due to the prevailing winds that flow west to east between North America and Europe.

After a rigorous series of test flights, Nungesser and Coli took off in their Levassseur PL8 biplane, named *Oiseau Blanc* (White Bird), on May 8, despite forecasts of poor weather over the North Atlantic. Next day, French newspapers triumphantly reported that the *Oiseau Blanc* had landed in New York. Celebrations erupted throughout France. But when confirmation failed to appear from North America, it became clear that this initial report was erroneous. As days passed without word of the fate of Nungesser and Coli, jubilation gave way to anxiety, fear, and, finally, despair. An extensive search by air over the ocean and along the coasts of Newfoundland and the eastern seaboard of North America turned up no evidence of the men or their machine.

This left the three US-led teams at Long Island to compete for the elusive prize. Many observers believed victory would go to Levine's single-engine monoplane, *Columbia,* because, in 1926, it had set an endurance record by flying for fifty-one hours without refuelling.

The *Columbia,* which was prepared for the New York-Paris flight by Bellanca, a highly accomplished aviation engineer, would likely have taken off first if not for a rivalry between two pilots vying to fly the plane. The dispute, which was widely reported in newspapers, reached its climax when Levine selected Clarence Chamberlin; the losing pilot, Lloyd Bertaud, responded by obtaining a court injunction that grounded the plane.

The Spirit of St Louis *(next page) may have looked flimsy while being pushed onto Roosevelt Field (below), but it proved sturdy enough to carry Charles "Lucky" Lindbergh to Paris (above right) in May 1927.*

This gave Lindbergh the time he needed to finish preparing his monoplane, *Spirit of St Louis*, built by the Ryan Airline Company of San Diego, California. Lindbergh also benefited from the misfortune experienced by Byrd, whose three-engine aircraft required a new series of time-consuming test flights following its accident.

On May 20, Lindbergh towed the *Spirit of St Louis* to Roosevelt Field; he then climbed into its cockpit and taxied down the runway. The plane — heavily laden with fuel — strained to take off, lurched unsteadily into the air, and barely avoided telephone wires near the end of the runway. Lindbergh flew northeast along the New England coast and Nova Scotia, before crossing over the easternmost region of North America, Newfoundland's Avalon Peninsula. In his Pulitzer Prize-winning book, *The Spirit of St Louis*, Lindbergh described the St John's he saw as he passed over the city:

I came upon it suddenly — the little city of St. John's, after skimming over the top of a creviced granite summit — flat-roofed houses and stores, nestled at the edge of a deep harbour.

It's almost completely surrounded by mountains. Further ahead, the entrance to the harbour is a narrow gap with sides running up steeply to the crest of a low coastal range, which holds back the ocean. Fishing boats are riding at buoys and men are at the wharves.

Twilight deepens as I plunge down into the valley. Mountains behind screen off the colours of the western sky. For me, this northern city is the last point on the last island of America — the end of land; the end of day … North America and its islands are behind. Ireland is two thousand miles [3,200 kilometres] away.

The most dangerous part of the journey came between Newfoundland and Ireland, where Lindbergh flew through fog and darkness. Icing also plagued the flight, and at times Lindbergh flew the aircraft just a few metres above the ocean waves in order to keep ice from forming on the wings. Once in daylight again, weather conditions improved, and more than 100,000 people were on hand to greet Lindbergh when the *Spirit of St Louis* landed at Le Bourget Airport in Paris. He had covered the 5,800-kilometre journey in thirty-three hours and thirty minutes, thereby becoming the first person to fly solo across the Atlantic. Lindbergh became an instant idol throughout Europe and North America, and was given star treatment during an official tour of the US. His competitors at Roosevelt and Curtiss airfields now had to content themselves with lesser honours.

Giuseppe Bellanca (on the left, with a mechanic) was an Italian immigrant to the US who became one of the world's leading aircraft engineers. He designed the Columbia *(seen below at Roosevelt Field in 1927), which lost the Orteig Prize to Charles Lindbergh. However, the* Columbia *was recognised as being a viable all-purpose aircraft rather than a plane built solely for a contest. Erroll Boyd, who in 1930 became the first Canadian to fly across the Atlantic, used the* Columbia — *renamed* Maple Leaf — *to reach Europe.*

Just two weeks later, Chamberlin proved that the *Columbia* could have won the Orteig Prize if Levine had not antagonised Bertaud. The court injunction was lifted on the same day as Lindbergh's history-making flight, and on June 4 Levine, with Chamberlin at the controls, took off from New York, bound for Berlin. The aircraft followed Lindbergh's route until reaching the European coast, but it ran out of fuel short of the German capital. Levine's dream of landing in triumph among thousands of cheering fans evaporated when Chamberlin was forced to land the plane in the German town of Eisleban. By then, however, the *Columbia* had already broken the non-stop distance record by flying 6,300 kilometres, 500 kilometres more than Lindbergh.

The *America* finally took off for Paris on June 29 with Bernt Balchen and Bertrand Acosta as pilots, George Noville as engineer, and Byrd as navigator. Although he had been beaten by Lindbergh and Levine, Byrd used his flight for scientific purposes, to test a theory that changes in wind speed and direction occur at different altitudes. He wanted to determine whether aircraft could fly faster by taking advantage of such wind patterns.

Byrd proved the validity of this supposition during the flight, as the aircraft made the fastest crossing yet of the Atlantic. Weather, however, would prevent Byrd and his crew from reaching Le Bourget Airport. Dense fog sent them off course over France, and the crew was forced to ditch the *America* onto a beach near the town of Le Havre after it ran out of fuel.

While much of North America and Europe revelled in the drama surrounding the New York-Paris race, Italians were engrossed by the feats of a pilot whose achievements had become a propaganda tool for Benito Mussolini's fascist regime. Francesco de Pinedo, an Italian air force pilot, became a national hero in 1925 after flying 54,700 kilometres over a period of several months in the South Pacific. This success would be followed in 1927 by a long-distance endurance test that offered even greater opportunities for demonstrating Italian flying prowess.

Pinedo and crewmen, co-pilot Carlo Del Prete and mechanic Vitale Zacchetti, left Italy in a Savoia-Marchetti SM-55 flying boat on a journey in 1927 that would cover over 46,600 kilometres and include four continents. The plane was christened *Santa Maria*, the name given to the flagship captained by the great Italian explorer, Christopher Columbus, in his voyage of discovery to America in 1492.

After leaving Italy, the *Santa Maria* touched down in Morocco, flew across the South Atlantic Ocean, and reached Brazil. The airmen travelled extensively throughout South America, including uncharted areas of the Amazon jungle, before turning north and flying to the US. When the *Santa Maria* arrived in New Orleans on March 29, it became the first foreign aircraft to fly into the United States.

The aviators then embarked on an extensive publicity tour of the US, with large crowds greeting the *Santa Maria* wherever it landed; but the marathon came to an abrupt halt when the aircraft caught fire during a refuelling stop at the Roosevelt Dam in Arizona. Nobody was injured in the blaze, which was the result of a carelessly discarded cigarette, but the famous plane was destroyed. This disaster did not put an end to Pinedo's journey, however. With Italy's national pride in the balance, Mussolini's Air Minister,

Famed polar adventurer Richard Byrd lost his chance to win the New York–Paris race when his aircraft crashed during a test flight. Byrd (on the right) with pilot Floyd Bennett (on the left) rebuilt the America. *It crossed the Atlantic, but ditched into the ocean on the coast of France.*

Francesco de Pinedo (below) fought for Italy during the First World War. In 1927, dictator Benito Mussolini supported Pinedo's four-continent tour in a Savoia-Marchetti SM-55 flying boat (above). It was dubbed Santa Maria, *the name given to the ship Christopher Columbus sailed to reach North America. The achievements of Pinedo and his crewmen, Carlo Del Prete and Vitale Zacchetti, were largely overshadowed by the publicity accorded Lindbergh.*

General Italo Balbo, ordered the construction of an identical replacement plane.

Thus far, the Italians had been welcomed as heroes at every stop. But many Italian Americans opposed Mussolini's brutal regime and viewed Pinedo as a willing tool of the dictatorship. Simmering resentment climaxed into street violence as Pinedo supporters and anti-fascist groups fought during a public reception for the aviators on April 26, 1927, in New York.

When the replica, named *Santa Maria II*, arrived in New York on board a ship in early May, Pinedo resumed his tour of the United States. By this time, however, the public had become distracted by the New York-Paris race, which had already cost the lives of six men. Because public attention was switching to competition for the Orteig Prize and away from the Italian marathon flight, Pinedo hoped to complete his return to Italy before a victor was declared in the New York-Paris competition. He intended to fly from Newfoundland to the Azores, and from there to Italy. Unfortunately for Pinedo, the *Santa Maria II* was unable to compete for the Orteig Prize because it lacked sufficient range to make a non-stop flight between North America and Europe.

Pinedo's bid to finish the tour before the Orteig Prize could be claimed was dashed, however, when poor weather grounded the *Santa Maria II* in Canada, first in Quebec and then in New Brunswick. Coincidentally, the day Pinedo flew into the Newfoundland community of Trepassey, on May 20, Lindbergh took off from New York and was himself flying over the island on the way to his historic transatlantic flight. Pinedo did not see the *Spirit of St Louis*, and left only a short, terse description of the barren landscape of the southern Avalon Peninsula surrounding Trepassey: "There was no sign of life but for a small fishing village."

The *Spirit of St Louis* passed over St John's while Pinedo was being driven to St John's in the company of C McKay Harvey, the Italian consul to Newfoundland. While in the country, Pinedo met numerous officials, and the government recognised his achievements by issuing overprinted postage stamps in his honour. Pinedo then returned to Trepassey, but rough waters delayed the departure of the *Santa Maria II* until May 23. The crew expected to fly directly to the Azores, but strong headwinds drained the aircraft of fuel and Pinedo was forced to land the seaplane in the vicinity of a fishing boat. The vessel towed the aircraft 320 kilometres to the Azores and, after the plane was repaired, Pinedo flew it back to the area where it had landed in the ocean. The crew then turned the *Santa Maria II* around and headed to Europe. Pinedo, Del Prete, and Zacchetti were greeted by a cheering throng of Italians when they landed in Ostia, west of Rome, on June 16, ending one of the longest flights to date.

Aircraft accidents later claimed the lives of two of the men: Del Prete died in a crash in 1928, and Pinedo was killed in 1933 when his plane caught fire during a takeoff from New York at the start of a planned non-stop flight to Baghdad.

Among the many people who were inspired by the Orteig Prize was Edward Schlee, the millionaire owner of the Wayco Oil Company, located in Detroit, Michigan. Schlee was largely responsible for the Newfoundland town of Harbour Grace becoming a focal point for early transatlantic aviators. An avid flyer, he had recently won an air race across the United States in a Stinson Detroiter monoplane.

Emboldened by this victory, Schlee hired pilot William Brock to join him in an attempt at setting a world record for circumnavigating the globe by air. They set an ambitious target of fifteen days to complete the journey, and Schlee decided that a stop in Newfoundland would be prudent in order to reduce the number of hours spent in the air between North America and Europe. He sent Fred Koehler, a representative of the Detroit-based Stinson Aircraft Corporation, to Newfoundland on a mission to find a suitable takeoff point and to build an airstrip. While in Newfoundland, Koehler met with a group of Harbour Grace residents who convinced him to locate the airstrip in their Conception Bay town by offering public funding for a portion of the construction costs.

Thanks to financial assistance from the Newfoundland government and a donation from Stinson, the non-profit Harbour Grace Airport Trust Company built a gravel airstrip measuring 1,220 metres long and 61 metres wide. Over the next decade this airfield would become the focal point for transatlantic aviation, until the late 1930s when it was supplanted by a new airport in central Newfoundland at Gander Lake.

Opposite: The decade-long pre-eminence of Harbour Grace as a port of call for transatlantic aviators ostensibly began with a world tour attempt by the Pride of Detroit. *Above: The crew of the* Pride of Detroit *(from left): William Brock and Edward Schlee, with two unidentified men.*

With the airstrip completed, on August 25 Schlee and Brock flew their Stinson Detroiter plane, named *Pride of Detroit*, to Harbour Grace from Old Orchard Beach, Maine. One day later, the aircraft took off for Europe and landed safely at Croydon, England, after a terrifying flight. Nearing Ireland, the *Pride of Detroit* encountered strong winds and rain that tossed the small plane about the night sky.

"The last few hours before dawn were our worst," Schlee wrote. "It seemed impossible that the airplane could live through such a storm. I kept thinking about my wife and two children in Detroit, wondering what they were doing. I even figured out what they probably were doing at that moment and I came to the conclusion they were doing what I was doing – praying."

Resuming their journey on September 1, Schlee and Brock reached Tokyo, Japan, two weeks later. Although their self-imposed fifteen-day deadline had passed, they decided to proceed with the last leg of their journey – crossing the formidable expanse of the Pacific Ocean. Traversing the Pacific by air was exceptionally hazardous in this era because navigational aids were relatively primitive and an aviator who became lost over the ocean would likely never be found alive.

Well aware of the risk, Schlee asked the US Navy to install a radio beacon on Midway Island, which would help him navigate from Tokyo to Honolulu. Meanwhile, American newspapers reported a complaint by Schlee that the Navy had refused to provide him and Brock with charts. This public rebuke drew the ire of Navy Secretary Curtis Wilbur, who reminded Schlee that charts were available to anybody at a cost of fifty cents each. More critical to Schlee and Brock

The Sir John Carling *(below), with pilots James Medcalf (upper left) and Terence Tully, disappeared after departing from Harbour Grace.*

was Wilbur's refusal to use government funds for installing a navigational aid on Midway Island.

"As long as I have anything to do with the Navy, it will do nothing to aid and abet men to commit suicide," Wilbur told the *New York Times*. With this, Schlee and Brock loaded the *Pride of Detroit* onto a freighter and returned by ship to the US.

In the weeks following the exploits of Lindbergh, Byrd, Levine, Pinedo, and the *Pride of Detroit*, several people, with varying degrees of experience, began plotting their own flights across the Atlantic. Despite the history of fatalities and accidents associated with flying across the Atlantic flights many of them downplayed the dangers posed by bad weather, unreliable equipment, navigational difficulties, and inadequate pilot training.

Late summer would prove to be the deadliest months for transatlantic hopefuls. Eight men and women were killed in this period alone, and with the carnage a public backlash against transoceanic flying arose in North America. September began with two aircraft leaving Canada's province of Ontario on a marathon race to England. One of them, the *Sir John Carling*, was sponsored by the Carling O'Keefe brewery, which offered CAD $25,000 for the first Canadian crew to fly non-stop from London, Ontario, to London, England. The brewery had advertised widely for competitors, but was able to attract only one qualifier because of its stipulation that an entrant had to own his own plane. That aspirant, Philip Wood, was subsequently disqualified when organisers learned he was an American. Carling O'Keefe then opted to purchase its own Stinson Detroiter monoplane and hire pilots for the flight. Two Ontario Provincial Air Service pilots, Terence Tully and James Medcalf, were selected.

Rather than return home, Wood decided to compete against Carling O'Keefe. He found a sponsor in Windsor, Ontario, and convinced an Iowa-born resident of Toronto, Clarence Schiller, to be his co-pilot. Like Tully and Medcalf, Schiller also flew with the Ontario Provincial Air Service. The men planned to fly non-stop from Windsor, Ontario, to Windsor, England, in Wood's Stinson Detroiter monoplane, which he named *Royal Windsor*.

On September 1, 1927, the race began with both the *Royal Windsor* and the *Sir John Carling* taking off on their race to England; however, the idea of a non-stop journey quickly proved to be wildly ambitious. Poor weather plagued the flights and both planes were forced to land far short of the British Isles. The *Royal Windsor* landed first near Montreal, Quebec, and then, two days later, at Portland, Maine. Thick fog forced Tully and Medcalf to make an unplanned

The demise of the Sir John Carling *and* Old Glory *convinced the crew of the* Royal Windsor *(opposite and below) to stop at Harbour Grace and abandon their transatlantic attempt.*

landing of the *Sir John Carling* near Caribou, Maine.

With these delays, the sponsors of both flights were compelled to revise their non-stop rules; Tully and Medcalf decided to launch their transatlantic flight from Harbour Grace, while Wood and Schiller opted to save time by skipping Newfoundland and flying non-stop to England from Maine. On September 5, after being delayed by fog in Maine, the *Sir John Carling* headed for the Newfoundland airstrip.

Wood and Schiller then revised their plans once again, this time deciding to fly eight kilometres to Old Orchard Beach, where they hoped to cross the ocean in tandem with another transatlantic aircraft. This would-be companion was a single-engine, German-made Fokker monoplane named *Old Glory*. The flight of the *Old Glory* was the dream of famed newspaper magnate William Randolph Hearst. His plan was to finance the first non-stop flight from New York to Rome, in hopes of attracting more subscribers to his New York newspaper, the *Daily Mirror*.

The pilot chosen for this venture, Lloyd Bertaud, was best known for preventing the *Columbia* from winning the Orteig Prize by obtaining a court order that forced Levine to keep it grounded. Hearst selected James Hill as navigator

and co-pilot for the transatlantic flight to Rome. Hill, who was one of the most experienced aviators in the United States, had been working as an airmail pilot.

Joining Bertaud and Hill was a passenger, Philip Payne, managing editor of the *Daily Mirror*. Canadian-born Payne had studied chemistry at the University of Toronto, and, after graduating, he moved to the United States, where he embarked on a career as a reporter. Like many of the journalists hired and promoted by Hearst, Payne was known for his tough investigative style. He was

also impetuous, and tended to rebuff authority — qualities that would prove disastrous as the *Old Glory* was readied for its Atlantic journey.

Although billed as a non-stop flight to Rome from New York, the *Old Glory* actually stopped at Old Orchard Beach to refuel after leaving Roosevelt Field on September 3. The change was made due to fears of the pilots and the plane's builder, Anthony Fokker, who argued that Roosevelt Field was too short to allow the plane to take off safely with a full load of fuel, in addition to Payne, who added an extra 90 kilograms to its weight.

The popular seaside vacation spot of Old

Orchard Beach, near Portland, had become a favoured departure point for aviators because it featured a natural runway: four kilometres of hard-packed beach sand. Here the *Old Glory* remained for three days while its crew waited for ideal weather conditions. But by the time the *Old Glory* had reached Maine, Hearst was reconsidering the whole venture. In mid-August, another Hearst-sponsored plane, the *Golden Eagle*, was lost in a race from California to Hawaii. Public criticism was mounting over such "stunt" flights, and Hearst did not relish the backlash that would result from possibly losing a second plane and the three men it carried. More ominous yet was the demise of the *San Rafael*, a sister aircraft of the *Old Glory*, which disappeared in late August on a transatlantic flight from England.

On September 5, Hearst telegraphed Payne in Old Orchard Beach, imploring his editor and the plane's crew to turn back. He even pledged to pay Bertaud and Hill their entire fee if they cancelled the flight. But Hearst neglected to issue a direct order prohibiting Payne and the pilots from flying. In their enthusiasm, the three men were unmoved by intimations of disaster.

Shortly after midday on September 6, the *Old Glory* took off from Old Orchard Beach, just four hours before the *Royal Windsor* arrived from nearby Portland. Wood and Schiller had thereby missed any chance they might have had to fly with the Hearst plane.

On board the *Old Glory* the pilots carried a wreath that they intended to drop into the ocean as a tribute to French pilots Nungesser and Coli, who had disappeared earlier that year. On the wreath was written, "Nungesser and Coli: You showed us the way. We followed. Bertaud, Payne and Hill." These words would be prophetic.

* *

Above: Public euphoria over the transatlantic feats of Lindbergh, the Columbia, *and the* America *soured after five aviators lost their lives within 24 hours in September 1927.* Old Glory *crashed into the ocean, killing all on board.*

Opposite: James Hill (left), passenger Philip Payne, and pilot Lloyd Bertaud.

* *

THE NEW YORK TIMES, WEDNESDAY, SEPTEMBER 7, 1927.

TRANSATLANTIC PLANE OLD GLORY AND HER CREW.

Old Glory on the beach at Old Orchard, Me., where she took off yesterday for Rome.

OLD GLORY PILOTS ARE VETERAN FLIER

Bertaud Made His First Hop in Glider When 12 Years Old, Crashing After 1,000 Feet.

HILL WAS STAR OF AIR MAIL

Made Night Flights for 2 Years in All Weathers Between Cleveland and Hadley Field.

Log of the Old Glory
On Her Flight to Rome

FOKKER CONFIDENT OF FLIGHT SUCCESS

Designer and Builder of Rome Plane Says Trip Will Lead to Regular Service.

The plane was spotted several times as it crossed Nova Scotia, the Gulf of St Lawrence, and the southeast coast of Newfoundland. Although it was flying low, in the range of 90 to 300 metres above the ocean, the *Old Glory* encountered ideal weather over the Gulf of St Lawrence, and the men reported by radio that they were making good time. But something then went terribly wrong. Shortly after 4:00 a.m. on September 7, the *Old Glory* sent out an SOS call. Six minutes later, a second call came from the plane: "Five hours from Newfoundland, bound east."

Because Bertaud and Hill were using dead reckoning to gauge direction, they were unable to give rescuers a precise coordinates about their location. Several ships conducted a search, but nothing was found. Worse still, no further messages were received from the stricken plane. Within an hour of the distress calls, the *Royal Windsor* took off for Harbour Grace. After missing a rendevous with the *Old Glory*, Wood and Schiller had decided to follow the route of the *Sir John Carling*, rather than attempt a direct flight to England from Maine.

It is not known whether Tully and Medcalf of the *Sir John Carling* had been told of the SOS call from the *Old Glory* or of the imminent arrival in Harbour Grace of their competitor, the *Royal Windsor*. By 7:00 a.m. on September 7 the *Sir John Carling* had taken off for England. The plane, which did not carry a radio, was never seen again.

These two disasters, combined with the recent deaths of another fifteen aviators over the Atlantic and Pacific oceans, resulted in calls for governments to outlaw such flights. Newspapers began referring to the ocean region between Newfoundland and Ireland as "The Atlantic Death Lane". T Douglas Robinson,

Press baron William Randolph Hearst's dream for boosting circulation for his newspaper empire turned into a nightmare when the crew of Old Glory plunged to their deaths off the coast of Newfoundland. Parts of the plane were recovered by a Newfoundland coastal steamer, the Kyle (above and opposite). The bodies of the three men were never found.

Acting Secretary of the US Navy, declared that overseas flights were a "nuisance bothering everybody", and that they served no useful purpose. This public pressure compelled Wood and Schiller to abandon their quest. Hearst offered a reward for the recovery of wreckage from the *Old Glory*. No bodies were found, but on September 12 several large pieces of wreckage were retrieved 800 kilometres east of Cape Race by the Newfoundland steamship *Kyle*.

After the *Sir John Carling* went missing, Carling O'Keefe officials claimed Tully and Medcalf had ignored requests by the company that they abandon their transatlantic flight, and said they had even offered to pay the pilots the full $25,000 prize for an unidentified future flying achievement. According to this account, the aviators refused, saying their honour was at stake and that they declined to accept this alternative. After the two men died, Carling O'Keefe gave the prize money to the families of the dead flyers.

Although the *Royal Windsor* never flew across the Atlantic, its pilots made an indelible contribution during their stay in Newfoundland. While driving back to Harbour Grace from an excursion to the city of St John's, they and a group of journalists stopped at a forest fire that was blocking the road in Kelligrews, a small town on the outskirts of the city. The visitors immediately began helping local volunteers fight the flames, which had engulfed several farmhouses. Wood, Schiller, and a photographer entered a burning home to rescue a blind man who was trapped in an upstairs room. After tying wet cloths over their faces, the three rescuers brought the man to safety. While flying back to Ontario from Newfoundland, Wood and Schiller dropped a wreath into the ocean in memory of those who had died while attempting to fly across the Atlantic. Schiller joined the Royal Canadian Air Force when war broke out in 1939, and flew bombers to Europe from Newfoundland with the Atlantic Ferry Command until his death, in a plane crash, in 1943.

In the decades following the drama of 1927, the deeds of those brave and colourful aviators who attempted transatlantic crossings that year have been largely forgotten. However, the careers and reputations of the three better-known figures who succeeded in flying non-stop to Europe from New York waxed and waned between the late 1920s and the Second World War.

Lindbergh's trajectory seemed limitless as he basked in the glory of winning the Orteig Prize; the story of his solo flight across the Atlantic made him a

national hero and today his name remains synonymous with the narrative of American individualism. During Lindbergh's lifetime, however, he sullied his reputation with anti-Semitic comments and by lobbying to keep the US out of the war.

Richard Byrd had already established himself as a pioneer prior to 1927, both as a scientist and as a pilot. During the war, Byrd designed instruments to assist seaplanes in making night-time landings; he followed this up in 1919 by leading the squadron of flying boats from Newfoundland to Europe in 1919.

After the war, Byrd turned to polar exploration, and in 1926 challenged Norwegian Roald Amundsen for the title of making the first flight over the North Pole. Amundsen, who had earned a stellar reputation by beating Robert Falcon Scott in an overland race to the South Pole in 1911, planned to fly over the North Pole in an Italian-built airship named the *Norge*. Both teams established camps on Spitsbergen, a Norwegian island north of the Arctic Circle. Byrd hoped to make a return flight between Spitsbergen and the North Pole, while Amundsen planned to fly over the Pole to Alaska.

Byrd and pilot Floyd Bennett took to the air first, and upon their return claimed to have flown over the Pole. Although Byrd initially reaped public adulation in the United States for this achievement, serious doubts were subsequently

Until the mid-1930s, airships and fixed-wing aircraft vied for pre-eminence. This competition was exemplified in 1926 by a race between Richard Byrd and Roald Amundsen for the honour of being the first to fly over the North Pole. Byrd, who flew the aircraft, was credited with victory, but serious doubts later emerged about his claim. Amundsen flew an airship, the Norge (above), to Alaska from Spitsbergen Island.

raised about the veracity of his claim. Many experts believed that the honour should belong to Amundsen, who flew the *Norge* to Alaska following Byrd's alleged success. Amundsen died in a plane crash near Spitsbergen in 1928 while searching for survivors of the *Italia*, an airship which had broken apart in an accident, killing many of the crew and stranding several survivors.

A year after his supposed polar flight, Byrd hoped to enhance his reputation in the New York-Paris competition, even though his plane was not an official participant. A series of delays, including an accident that injured Byrd and badly damaged the *America*, forced him to postpone his attempt. This gave Lindbergh the time he needed to carry out his historic flight, and again Byrd was denied the accolades he believed should have been his. Worse yet, questions were posed about Byrd's competence after his plane ditched into the ocean over France, since as navigator he was primarily responsible for the aircraft becoming lost in a fog bank.

Byrd then turned his attention to Antarctica, starting in 1929 when he achieved the first flight over the South Pole, along with pilot Bernt Balchen of Norway. Balchen had flown with Byrd on the *America* flight two years earlier. His five expeditions to Antarctica resulted in the discovery of thousands of square kilometres of territory, all of which were claimed for the United States. Byrd's dedication to the scientific study of Antarctica included spending the winter of 1934 in the interior of the frozen continent, where he collected data that became critical to the understanding its climate.

Charles Levine, one of Byrd's main competitors in the New York-Paris race, was one of the most colourful promoters of aviation in the 1920s. The son of a New York scrap-metal dealer, Levine made his fortune after obtaining a contract with the US War Department in 1917 for the buying and disposal of shell casings.

In the mid-1920s, he and aircraft designer Giuseppe Bellanca formed Columbia Aircraft Company, which began manufacturing planes. The *Columbia*, which Levine and pilot Clarence Chamberlin flew to Germany in 1927, was hailed as the most technologically advanced aircraft of its day.

Levine appeared to thrive on publicity, and frequently attracted controversy. In one notable instance, at a Chicago casino in 1928, Levine, who was accompanied by Mabel Boll, a socialite known as the "Diamond Queen", punched a newspaper editor who had written an unfavourable article about him. The New *York Times* reported: "When the dust cleared, Miss Boll, sparkling with diamonds as usual, took Levine's arm and led him away." Boll accompanied Levine on a flight to Cuba in March 1928, in the *Columbia*, and she borrowed his plane for a transatlantic attempt of her own two months later. Levine lost heavily in the stock market crash of 1929, but continued spending money on experimental aircraft.

Trouble rarely strayed from Levine's side, but until the mid-1930s he managed to avoid significant legal difficulties. This changed in 1937, when he was convicted on charges of smuggling tungsten to the United States from Canada; he served two years in jail for the crime.

Levine's soiled reputation would undergo a dramatic turnaround during the Second World War, however, as he demonstrated a degree of courage and self-lessness that had not previously been evident. In 1942, he was again convicted of smuggling, but this time it was for bringing a German citizen into the United States from Mexico. Even though the German turned out to be a refugee from a concentration camp, Levine was sentenced to 150 days in jail. The Columbia Aircraft Company was sold shortly after the Second World War, and Levine died in 1991 at the age of ninety-four.

· ·

Charles Levine (left) was typical of the flamboyant risk-takers who financed and flew planes across the world's continents and oceans during the 1920s and 1930s. Levine is seen here with "Diamond Queen" Mabel Boll and pilot Bertrand Acosta.

· ·

Glamour mixed easily with the drama of aviation in the 1920s. Socialite Mabel Boll (centre left) became the centre of attention in Harbour Grace when she landed there in 1928 with the intention of becoming the first woman to fly across the Atlantic. However, Amelia Earhart denied her that honour, and Boll is now largely forgotten.

CHAPTER 3

WOMEN TAKE FLIGHT

The swashbuckling image of aviators, personified by Charles Lindbergh, inspired many flyers with varying levels of experience to attempt their own transatlantic heroics in the months following his achievement in May 1927. Many of these ventures ended in failure and, often, death.

Although men dominated the world of flight during the pioneer era, many women shared their dreams. In the mid-1920s and throughout the 1930s, they too would share both the glory and the tragedy. The goal of following Lindbergh and becoming the first female to make a non-stop crossing of the Atlantic lured several women to follow his lead.

In August 1927, Anne Lowenstein-Wertheim, a wealthy, adventure-seeking

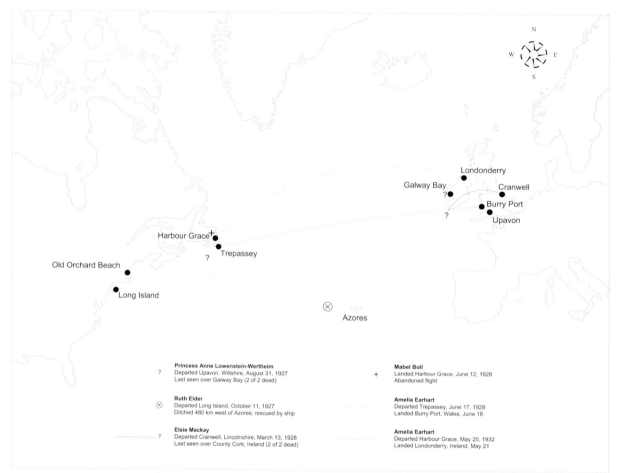

Princess Anne Lowenstein-Wertheim
Departed Upavon, Wiltshire, August 31, 1927
Last seen over Galway Bay (2 of 2 dead)

Ruth Elder
Departed Long Island, October 11, 1927
Ditched 480 km west of Azores; rescued by ship

Elsie Mackay
Departed Cranwell, Lincolnshire, March 13, 1928
Last seen over County Cork, Ireland (2 of 2 dead)

Mabel Boll
Landed Harbour Grace, June 12, 1928
Abandoned flight

Amelia Earhart
Departed Trepassey, June 17, 1928
Landed Burry Port, Wales, June 18

Amelia Earhart
Departed Harbour Grace, May 20, 1932
Landed Londonderry, Ireland, May 21

sixty-two-year-old aristocrat, made the first attempt. Born Anne Saville, daughter of the English Count of Mexborough, she became a princess by marrying a German prince, Ludwig Karl.

Her husband's early death allowed the princess the freedom to indulge her love for travel and aviation. In 1912, she became one of the first women to fly across the English Channel, and she later made long-distance flights throughout Europe and as far south as Egypt. In 1927, the princess decided to fly from England to Harbour Grace, Newfoundland, and from there to the Canadian capital, Ottawa. She acquired a single-engine Fokker monoplane and hired two Imperial Airways pilots, Frederick Minchin and Leslie Hamilton, to be her crew. The aircraft, named *St Raphael* (a patron saint of travellers), took off from Upavon, Wiltshire, on August 31 after being blessed by the Bishop of Cardiff. The crew of a ship spotted it flying slowly over Galway Bay, Ireland, and heading west, but the *St Raphael* and its crew were never seen again.

In October 1927, a glamorous American film actress, Ruth Elder, made her

Princess Lowenstein-Wertheim (right)
hired two pilots to fly her across the treach-
erous westward route across the Atlantic.
Their aircraft was last spotted over the
North Atlantic before it disappeared.
Another victim of the North Atlantic was
Frances Grayson (below), who died while
flying a Sikorsky aircraft from New York to
England. American pilot and film actress
Ruth Elder (next page) was luckier: she
and pilot George Haldeman were rescued
from the ocean by a ship after ditching their
plane during their transatlantic attempt.

she hired pilot George Haldeman to fly with her to Europe from New York. Elder's sponsors acquired a Stinson Detroiter aircraft, which she named *American Girl*. Unlike Lowenstein-Wertheim, Elder opted for the longer southern route, via the Azores, in order to avoid poor weather over the North Atlantic during the autumn months. However, a leaking fuel line forced Haldeman and Elder to ditch their aircraft into the ocean 480 kilometres west of the Azores. They landed in a shipping lane and were rescued. Despite coming short of their goal, Elder and Haldeman were awarded a tickertape parade in New York.

Elder's failure meant that there was now an opportunity for a New York real estate agent and former newspaper reporter, Frances Grayson, who had been preparing for several months to make the ocean crossing. Although Grayson had no experience as a pilot, Lindbergh's success had inspired her to obtain an aircraft and hire a crew to fly her to England from New York.

A strong believer in equal rights for women, Grayson was quoted as saying:

> I am going to be the first woman across the Atlantic, and mine the only ship since Lindbergh's to reach its destination. I will prove that woman can compete with man in his own undertakings.

With financial assistance from Aage Ancker, daughter of a Pittsburgh steel manufacturer, Grayson purchased a new Sikorsky-made amphibious aircraft, which she named *Dawn*. Several experienced pilots either declined to fly the plane, or left Grayson's team, particularly when the *Dawn* lost an engine during a test flight, and proved incapable of taking off with a full load of fuel. Eventually Oskar Omdal, a Norwegian, agreed to fly the plane, although Grayson planned to take turns at the controls. The crew also included navigator Brice Goldsborough, and radio engineer Frank Koehler, who had overseen preparation of the Harbour Grace airfield a few months earlier for the *Pride of Detroit*.

Rather than follow the safer but longer mid-Atlantic route taken by Elder, Grayson opted to gamble with the harsh winter conditions off the east coast of Newfoundland. After several months of delays the *Dawn* left Curtiss Field on December 23, bound for Harbour Grace. From there Grayson intended to complete what she expected would be a historic flight to London.

However, after leaving New York, and flying across the eastern seaboard of the US and Nova Scotia, the plane and its four occupants were never seen again. Reports suggested that the aircraft's engines were heard over the Newfoundland communities of Old Perlican, Harbour Breton, and Heart's Content, but these claims were never proved.

The mounting death toll among transatlantic aviators failed to deter a second English aristocrat from trying her luck at becoming the first woman to fly across the ocean. Not only did Elsie Mackay, daughter of the Earl of Inchcape, decide to fly the treacherous westward route with its strong headwinds, she chose to make her attempt in late winter, when weather conditions over the North Atlantic are particularly hazardous.

Elsie Mackay (left) won plaudits for her acting, and notoriety for her lifestyle. After she disappeared during a transatlantic attempt in 1927, her co-pilot's widow, Emilie Hinchliffe (right), claimed she had received a message — through a medium — from her husband. Her daughter, Jean, is clutching a toy given to her by another controversial aviator, Charles Levine.

Mackay was a stage and film actress whose name had become tinged by scandal. In 1917, at the age of twenty-four, she married a serviceman she had met while working as a hospital nurse. Lord Inchcape had objected to the marriage, and temporarily cut off all financial support to his daughter. Four years later the marriage was annulled after a highly publicised court case.

As Mackay learned to fly, she became known for her daring. While training for her pilot's certificate in 1922, she had flown a plane so recklessly that her restraining belt snapped during an unplanned mid-air roll. If the instructor had not grabbed her, she would have fallen from the cockpit and plummeted to her death.

Lord Inchcape, who owned a large shipping firm, tried to rein in his thrill-seeking daughter by making her the artistic director of his steamship company. In this position she was responsible for cabin décor and kitchen design in her father's passenger vessels. She also became an advisor to the British Empire Air League.

But Mackay refused to settle down, and in the midst of international excitement over Lindbergh and his competitors she decided to become the first woman to fly across the Atlantic. In 1928, she hired an experienced pilot, Walter Hinchliffe, and gave him money to purchase a Stinson Detroiter aircraft. It was identical to the *Pride of Detroit*, which had flown to Europe from Newfoundland a year earlier. She named her plane *Endeavour* and planned to fly to Harbour Grace from England.

Mackay's father strongly opposed her intentions, so she publicly stated that Hinchliffe's friend, Gordon Sinclair, would accompany him. Mackay emphatically denied that she would fly in the *Endeavour*.

Only after the plane took off from Cranwell airport in Lincolnshire on March 13 did the public learn that Mackay, not Sinclair, was flying with Hinchliffe. The *Endeavour* was spotted flying over the coast of County Cork, Ireland, and then by ships at sea. It disappeared, however, and the wreckage was never found.

In November of that year, Hinchliffe's widow, Emilie, told an audience in London that, through a medium, she had received a message from her dead husband describing the last hours of his final flight.

"After leaving the Irish coast I flew in a northwesterly direction," she said he had told her. "We then got into the force of a storm. The gale was terrible. It broke one strut of the machine and another strut cracked. The canvass was tearing and one plug in the engine missing ... At three a.m. the machine came down within sight of the Azores. I trust some parts of the machine will be found near the rocks mentioned."

The notoriety that had dogged Elsie Mackay was to follow Lord Inchcape in the weeks following his daughter's death. To honour her memory he had established a £500,000 Elsie Mackay Trust Fund, which was to be administered by the British government. Emilie Hinchliffe then complained that Inchcape had refused her request for money to support herself and her three children. As public pressure mounted, Inchcape agreed to give her the equivalent of US $50,000.

This deadly series of failures by women to fly across the Atlantic would end in June 1928 with a showdown in Newfoundland between two very different personalities. One aspirant, Amelia Earhart, was already an accomplished, but little-known, pilot. Earhart was born in Kansas in 1897, and she became entranced with aviation in 1917 while serving as a nursing assistant to servicemen recuperating at a hospital near an airfield in Toronto, Ontario. After earning her pilot's licence in 1922 and purchasing a plane, Earhart set an altitude record for women of 4.2 kilometres and competed in several aircraft races. Financial difficulties then forced her to sell the plane, although she found a job as a social worker and was able to support herself.

In 1927, while working in Boston, Earhart received an offer that gave her the chance to rejoin the world of aviation. An American heiress, Amy (Phipps)

• •

Below: The Friendship, *moored in Trepassey harbour.*
Opposite top: Amelia Earhart caused a sensation in Harbour Grace as she prepared her Lockheed Vega for a solo flight across the Atlantic in 1932. She and two reporters discuss the upcoming flight. To her left are Lewis Esperance and mechanic Ed Gorski.

• •

Guest, was funding what she hoped would be the first transatlantic flight by a woman. Guest, who had married former British Air Minister, Frederick Guest, had obtained a three-engine Fokker aircraft from Richard Byrd, which she named *Friendship*.

Guest hired publicist George Putnam to find two male crew who would fly the plane and a woman to travel with them as a passenger. She stipulated that the woman be American, a pilot, well-educated, physically attractive, and possess good manners. Earhart, who was known to Putnam, accepted the job, even though she would only be flying as a passenger.

On June 4, 1928, Earhart, along with pilot Wilmer Stultz — who had resigned as Grayson's pilot a year earlier — and mechanic Louis Gordon, landed in the southern Newfoundland town of Trepassey. They had started the journey in Old Orchard Beach, Maine, and stopped at Halifax, Nova Scotia, en route. The trio expected to take off for Europe from Trepassey the day after their arrival, but high winds and fog delayed their departure. They would become guests of the people of Trepassey for nearly two weeks.

Competing with Earhart was flamboyant New York socialite and cabaret performer, Mabel Boll. Known as "The Diamond Queen", Boll was romantically involved with millionaire playboy Charles Levine. Levine had already set an aviation record in 1927 when he flew as a passenger with pilot Clarence Chamberlin from New York to Germany in the *Columbia*. In March 1928, Boll and Levine had flown as passengers with the *Columbia* on the first non-stop flight to Havana, Cuba, from New York.

Levine agreed to loan Boll the *Columbia* for a transatlantic flight in which she would be a passenger. Boll had expected Stultz to be her pilot, since he had flown her and Levine on the record-setting Havana flight. She became incensed when Stultz agreed to fly with Earhart and the *Friendship* instead. "I can't understand it," Boll complained. "Now he has taken off with this other woman, and I was sure he would fly with me. I depended on him."

Boll responded by hiring a replacement pilot, Oliver Le Boutillier, and a mechanic, Arthur Argles. She had been delayed in starting her flight from New York, but, fortunately for her, poor weather in Trepassey had grounded Earhart. The *Columbia*, with Boll and her crew, flew to Harbour Grace from New York on June 12.

Like Earhart, Boll anticipated only a short stop in Harbour Grace before taking off for Europe. However, the fog and high winds that grounded the *Friendship* also prevented the *Columbia* from leaving. Boll was compelled to find other activities to keep her busy until the skies cleared. The Knights of Columbus threw a reception for the crew of the *Columbia*, and they were fêted by dignitaries during a tour of St John's.

In contrast, Earhart, Stultz, and Gordon never strayed far from their aircraft. Having been unprepared for a lengthy stay in Trepassey, and arriving with only the clothes they were wearing, the three aviators were forced to buy or borrow clothing from local residents.

Earhart wrote that "[t]he flannel nightgown ... was borrowed and I began to feel that even its sturdy fabric would be worn out before we ever got away from Trepassey — although I didn't know about the wearing qualities of flannel gowns, never having had one before. Incidentally, its warmth was supplemented by the down beds upon which we slept and into which we sank luxuriously."

Their time in Trepassey was largely spent playing cards, fishing, and sightseeing. Music proved to be an activity that brought visitors and residents together, and Earhart described how local people would gather outside the fence of their boarding house whenever an instrument was being played.

Finally, on June 17, after several aborted attempts at taking off, the *Friendship* rose from Trepassey harbour. Under the command of Stultz, and carrying only essential equipment and little food or water, the plane flew across the North Atlantic with Ireland as its destination.

Fog shrouded the *Friendship* throughout much of the trip, and navigation became more difficult after its radio broke down. The plane became lost as they neared Europe and, with only one hour of fuel remaining, they decided to land at the first opportunity. This happened to be Burry Port, a coastal town in Wales. The initial reaction to the *Friendship* from local residents was mild curiosity, but this changed to frenzied excitement once word spread that the plane had crossed the Atlantic and that one of its occupants was a woman.

When news arrived that the *Friendship* had taken off, and then that Earhart had won the race to be the first woman to cross the ocean by air, the disappointment was too much for Boll. She donated US $500 to the operators of the Harbour Grace airstrip and flew with the *Columbia* back to New York.

After the successful flight by the *Friendship*, the two women's lives veered in radically different directions. Unlike Earhart, whose transatlantic journey gave her an opportunity to proceed with a career in aviation, Boll soon lost interest in flying. For a few years, her tempestuous lifestyle and associations with wealthy men such as Levine kept her name in New York newspapers. Boll would marry five times throughout her life; her husbands included a South African plantation owner, a Polish count, and a musician with the New York Philharmonic Orchestra. Boll, who was rarely seen in public without her diamonds, once conceded that she loved

● ●

Next page: In 1932 Amelia Earhart became the first woman, and the second person since Lindbergh, to fly solo across the Atlantic. She followed this achievement by setting speed and distance records in the Pacific Ocean. Earhart is seen atop her Lockheed Vega after completing a non-stop solo flight from Hawaii to Oakland, California, in 1935. Inset: Officers of the passenger liner, President Roosevelt, with Louis Gordon (second from right) and Wilmer Stultz (fourth from right), listen as Earhart reads a congratulatory telegram during their triumphant return to the United States.

● ●

Mabel Boll, seen here in Harbour Grace, lost her bid to become the first woman to make a non-stop crossing by air to Europe from North America.

jewels more than men. "There is no pleasure in the world comparable to the possession of diamonds," she said. Boll suffered tragedy in 1942 when her only child, a son, died of appendicitis. In 1949 she was committed to a Manhattan mental hospital. She died there that year, apparently of a stroke.

In contrast with Boll, Earhart's celebrity status continued to grow. In 1928, the public in both North America and Europe clamoured to learn more about the woman who had conquered the Atlantic. She was dubbed "Lady Lindy", in part due to her physical resemblance to Lindbergh.

But Earhart felt uncomfortable taking credit for the flight. She downplayed her role and emphasised that Stultz and Gordon had actually flown the plane:

I was a passenger on the journey — just a passenger. Everything that was done to bring us across was done by Wilmer Stultz and 'Slim' Gordon. Any praise I can give them they ought to have.

Earhart would later note that while Stultz received payment of US $20,000 and Gordon US $5,000, she was required to turn over the fees she received from writing accounts of the journey to the flight's promoters.

This sense of having unfinished business spurred Earhart to prepare for another crossing of the Atlantic, in 1932, but this time with herself at the controls. This flight, and other achievements throughout the mid-1930s, would establish her as an icon of human achievement.

Earhart was determined to demonstrate that female pilots were as capable as men at flying. To prove her point, she would mark the fifth anniversary of Lindbergh's 1927 New York–Paris flight by making her own solo transatlantic journey to Paris.

In the early hours of May 20 — the anniversary of Lindbergh's transatlantic flight — Bernt Balchen flew Earhart and mechanic Ed Gorski to Harbour Grace from Roosevelt Field, Long Island. Balchen, who gained valuable experience flying across the Atlantic with Richard Byrd in 1927, was instrumental in assisting Earhart in preparing for her own solo journey.

Earhart slept five hours at a Harbour Grace hotel before climbing into the cockpit of her single-engine Lockheed Vega aircraft. Hotel proprietor, Rose Archibald, gave her a thermos of soup moments before she took off for Paris.

Difficulties plagued her throughout the journey, starting with failure of the altimeter. She then flew into a severe lightning storm and was pushed off course. More serious yet, a weld in the exhaust manifold split open. During the night, flames from fuel combustion shot brilliantly into the darkness.

Later, the Vega flew into dense cloud. As she climbed to escape, a film of ice appeared on the aircraft's wings. Suddenly, the plane began spiralling down to the ocean. Fortunately, as it reached the warmer air below, the ice melted, allowing Earhart to regain control and pull the plane out of its dive. She later wrote:

How long I spun I do not know. As we righted and held level again, through the blackness I could see the whitecaps, too close for comfort.

More unnerving yet, fuel began leaking onto her shoulder from the cabin fuel gauge. This leak, combined with the widening split in the exhaust manifold, posed a significant fire risk, so Earhart decided to land at the first opportunity rather than continue on to Paris. She came to earth in a pasture near Londonderry, Northern Ireland.

Earhart came short of reaching France, but to the public that hardly mattered. Huge crowds followed her in London after she flew to the British capital from Ireland. Unlike many pilots of her era, Earhart downplayed the importance of the flight to the progress of aviation. Instead, she used her achievement to champion women's rights. She told journalists in London:

Outside of demonstrating that a woman can fly the Atlantic alone, I don't see that I have added anything to the science of aviation or anything else. But if I've helped break through the barriers of the tradition that women are helpless, that's something, isn't it?

Earhart's feminism was radical for her time, and she used her status to advance this philosophy. In September 1932, Earhart was part of a delegation from the National Woman's Party that met President Herbert Hoover to urge his support for legislation guaranteeing equal rights to women. She also believed that women could, in some situations, be physically stronger than men — a theory tested, and partially proven, during the early years of the American space program. "Woman really is capable of standing strain better and longer than man," Earhart said.

Earhart looked forward to the day when she would fly on passenger aircraft across the world's oceans. She would never realise that dream. In 1937, she and navigator Fred Noonan took off from Oakland, California, on a round-the-world journey. They followed a route close to the equator, and hoped to better the time of another American aviator, Wiley Post, who had set the record in 1931.

Flying east, they arrived in New Guinea on June 29. From there Earhart planned to fly to tiny Howland Island 3,500 kilometres away, the longest over-water leg of the trip. She and Noonan were unable to find the island, and they disappeared. Numerous attempts have been made in the ensuing decades to find remains of Earhart and her plane. In 2010 a team of archeologists suggested that bone fragments and artifacts found on Nikumaroro Island in the Pacific could have belonged to Earhart, although this evidence is so far inconclusive.

Aviation royalty in Atlantic City, New Jersey, on August 2, 1933. A swimming party was given for husband and wife flyers, Amy Johnson (seated, right) and James Mollison (right), by Amelia Earhart and her husband, George Putnam (left). Mollison had recently suffered minor injuries when he and Johnson crash-landed their plane after achieving a successful westerly crossing of the Atlantic.

Dedicated to Fitzmaurice, Von Hue

SKY-B

by August Jos

CHAPTER 4

THE LUCKY AND
THE FOOLHARDY

Composers sometimes wrote music to celebrate well-known aviators, in this case the crew of the Bremen, which, in 1928, achieved the first westerly crossing of the Atlantic.

I f anybody believed that the carnage of 1927 would dampen enthusiasm among aviators for flying across the Atlantic, they were mistaken. Indeed, enthusiasts in North America and Europe watched with envy as Charles Lindbergh basked in the glow of public adulation and grew rich in an avalanche of endorsement contracts.

Many aviators dismissed the plethora of accidents and deaths that followed Lindbergh's achievement as being the product of bad luck, inexperience, or poor planning. The east-west route was particularly hazardous to fliers, because aircraft flying from Europe to North America must contend with powerful prevailing winds that flow west to east across the Atlantic, conditions that slow progress through the skies and force planes to use more fuel.

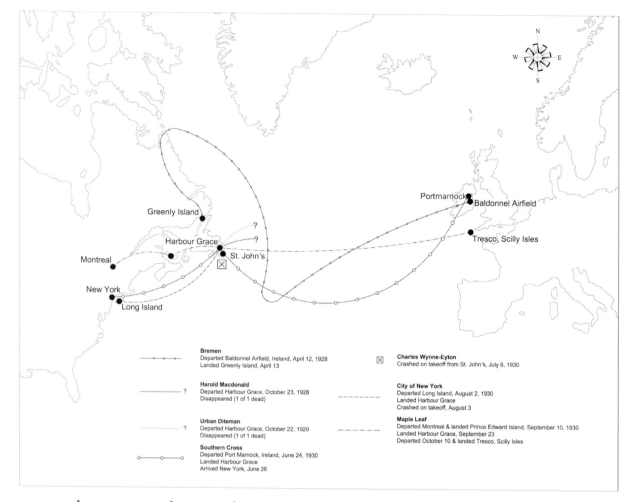

Bremen
Departed Baldonnel Airfield, Ireland, April 12, 1928
Landed Greenly Island, April 13

Harold Macdonald
Departed Harbour Grace, October 23, 1928
Disappeared (1 of 1 dead)

Urban Diteman
Departed Harbour Grace, October 22, 1929
Disappeared (1 of 1 dead)

Southern Cross
Departed Port Marnock, Ireland, June 24, 1930
Landed Harbour Grace
Arrived New York, June 26

Charles Wynne-Eyton
Crashed on takeoff from St. John's, July 6, 1930

City of New York
Departed Long Island, August 2, 1930
Landed Harbour Grace
Crashed on takeoff, August 3

Maple Leaf
Departed Montreal & landed Prince Edward Island, September 10, 1930
Landed Harbour Grace, September 23
Departed October 10 & landed Tresco, Scilly Isles

In 1927, several aviators disappeared going this direction, among them Charles Nungesser and Elsie Mackay. Nevertheless, many Europeans were determined to conquer the Atlantic from their own shores, among them a German-led team expedition that was determined to etch its name in the history of flight.

Certainly, the risks of flying this route failed to deter Baron Guenther von Hünefeld, a wealthy German aristocrat, who was inspired to cross the Atlantic by Lindbergh's New York–Paris flight.

He purchased a German-made Junkers W33 and named it *Bremen*. Hünefeld was not a pilot, however, so he hired Hermann Köhl, a former First World War airman who had become chief pilot for Luft Hansa (which was renamed Lufthansa in 1933). This 1928 bid was not their first attempt at crossing the Atlantic. In August 1927, Köhl and Hünefeld were forced to abandon their initial flight after battling strong headwinds for twenty-four hours after taking off from Germany.

With this unsuccessful attempt, they were forced to wait until the following year before trying again. This time, however, they would not go alone. On March 26, 1928 they flew the *Bremen* to Baldonnel Airfield, an airfield near Dublin. Here, Köhl and Hünefeld were joined by a senior officer in Ireland's air force, James Fitzmaurice.

Fitzmaurice, who was born in Dublin in 1898 and spent much of his childhood in the town of Portlaoise, and his early adult years in the armed forces. At age sixteen, with the outset of the First World War Fitzmaurice attempted to joined the armed forces in Ireland; however, his father had him withdrawn because of his age.

A year later, in 1915, Fitzmaurice was old enough to enlist with the British Army, and was soon sent to fight in France. After being injured during combat, he was recommended for an officer's commission and served as a lieutenant with the army. In 1918, Fitzmaurice completed his pilot training, but the Armistice was declared before he could take part in battle. He continued to serve with the Royal Air Force, but switched to the Irish Army Air Corps in 1922 after Ireland gained independence from Great Britain. Fitzmaurice was rapidly promoted, until becoming commandant of the Air Corps in 1927.

Like Köhl and Hünefeld, Fitzmaurice was inspired by Lindbergh's flight to Paris in 1927, and that autumn he attempted his own transatlantic journey. In September, he and co-pilot Robert McIntosh took off from Ireland in a monoplane, manufactured by the Dutch Fokker Aircraft Company, which he named *Princess Xenia*. However, after flying for several hours, they were forced to return due to strong headwinds.

Fitzmaurice agreed to fly with the Germans the following year, in 1928. However, the three men may have wondered whether history was being repeated as they waited for skies to clear over the North Atlantic in March and April. Poor weather kept the *Bremen* grounded for seventeen days at Baldonnel Airfield until the early morning of April 12 when conditions were judged favourable for flying across the ocean. The *Bremen* rose into the sky and set a course for Mitchel Field, an airfield in Garden City, Long Island.

The *Bremen* would never reach New York. Nothing was heard from the plane after it cleared the coast of Ireland, since radio had not been brought on board because the added weight would have increased fuel consumption. As the hours passed, it seemed as though the *Bremen* had disappeared like so many of its predecessors.

But then, after two days of silence from the missing plane, a telegraph message was transmitted to the world from Point Amour, a tiny village located on the south coast of Labrador. On April 13, after thirty-five hours in the air, the plane had crash-landed at Greenly Island, Quebec, a barren, treeless outcrop in the Strait of Belle Isle midway between northeastern Quebec, Labrador and the west coast of Newfoundland.

All three men aboard the plane emerged uninjured after the *Bremen* landed on a frozen pond and crashed through the ice. Their story of flying blindly through fog and stormy weather — and of how they risked death in landing on a rocky island — would captivate the public through newspapers, magazines, radio broadcasts, and newsreels.

According to the men, the flight had gone well until nightfall, as the *Bremen* approached the Grand Banks area east of Newfoundland. Here, the plane encountered a thick, wide-ranging fog bank. Not only were Köhl and Fitzmaurice unable to guide the aircraft by the stars, but in the fading light they also found it difficult to use the compass.

The pilots fought against wind, rain, snow, and fog as they flew blindly through the night. As the sun rose, the fog began to clear and the three men found themselves travelling along the coast of northern Labrador, heading into the Arctic. Realizing that they were off course, they turned the *Bremen* south and followed the Torngat Mountains and Lake Melville.

At about noon, through a gap in the cloud cover, they sighted what appeared to be a ship, but by now, the *Bremen* was running low on fuel and the men were running out of both time and options. Despite the danger, they decided to land in the water and await rescue. Upon descending, however, the men discovered that what they were looking at was

The crash-landing of the Bremen *on Greenly Island (opposite left) set a record, but also left the aircraft too badly damaged to take off again. The flyers — (below left to right) Baron Guenther von Hünefeld, James Fitzmaurice, and Hermann Köhl — escaped without injury and were fêted in a tickertape parade in New York after their rescue.*

actually a lighthouse on Greenly Island.

In their desperation, Köhl and Fitzmaurice had no choice but to risk death by crash-landing. As the plane landed, the wheels sank into a peat bog, damaging the aircraft beyond repair, but the men were safe.

The flyers soon received excellent care from a group of seven families who were living on Greenly Island and working at a fishing station owned by Job Brothers, a Newfoundland fish trading company. Telegraph stations on the south coast of Labrador were alerted to the arrival of the Bremen. After that, news of the flyers' landing quickly spread around the world, and a race to Greenly Island by the largest newspapers in North America immediately ensued. But getting to the island proved to be almost as difficult as the flight of the *Bremen* itself. Pack ice had blocked the Strait of Belle Isle, and even a Canadian icebreaker was unable to reach the island.

On April 15, a flight sponsored by the *Toronto Daily Star* was the first to arrive on Greenly Island. Its pilot, Clarence Schiller, had flown with Robert Wood on an aborted Atlantic crossing by the *Royal Windsor* in 1927. Schiller, who was acting as a reporter for the *Star*, was among sixty journalists who would make the difficult journey to Greenly Island.

One of those caught in the media frenzy was Floyd Bennett, the pilot credited with flying Richard Byrd over the North Pole in 1926. Bennett and Bernt Balchen, who flew the *America* in a transatlantic crossing in 1927, were hired by the *New York World* newspaper to fly spare parts to repair the *Bremen*.

Bennett had been recuperating in hospital following a recent air crash when he was asked to fly to Greenly Island. Despite his fragile condition, he agreed; however, during the 1,600-kilometre flight he contracted pneumonia and was rushed to a hospital in Quebec City. As Bennett's condition worsened, Charles Lindbergh flew non-stop to Quebec City from New York, carrying medication to save his life. But Lindbergh was too late to save his friend, and as a tribute, Byrd named the plane that took him over the South Pole in 1929 after Bennett. An airport in Brooklyn, New York, was also named in his honour.

At Greenly Island, attempts at repairing the *Bremen* proved unsuccessful. Köhl, Hünefeld, and Fitzmaurice were finally flown from the island, almost two weeks after their landing. A tickertape parade held for the flyers four days later attracted two million people along a sixteen-kilometre route. They followed this with a tour of the American northeast, as well as Montreal, Quebec City, Germany, and Ireland. Hünefeld, who completed a flight throughout Southeast Asia in September later that year, died in 1929 from tuberculosis.

Fitzmaurice left the Irish Air Corps in 1929, and worked in the United States during the 1930s. He returned to Ireland after the Second World War and died in 1965.

The fate of the *Bremen* differed markedly from most transatlantic bids that had gone wrong in that the flyers were rescued. Others were not so lucky, including many who had followed the *Pride of Detroit* by using Harbour Grace as their departure point for crossing the ocean by air. The dangers of attempting this feat are illustrated by a sobering statistic: by mid-1928 only one of the five aircraft that had used Harbour Grace as a departure point for Europe had been successful. The *Pride of Detroit* managed to reach England, but the *Sir John Carling* disappeared. Three other flights – Admiral Mark Kerr's *Atlantic* in 1919, the *Royal Windsor* in

1927, and Mabel Boll's *Columbia* in June 1928 – had been abandoned.

However, this dismal record failed to deter those who shared Lindbergh's dream, and in October 1928 Harbour Grace would host another bid for a flight across the Atlantic. Harold MacDonald, an Englishman who had served in the Royal Navy during the First World War, arrived by ship in St John's, Newfoundland, on September 23. MacDonald, who had recently retired from the navy, only learned to fly a year earlier. Immediately after obtaining his pilot's licence MacDonald embarked upon a flight from Great Britain to India, despite accumulating only ten hours' experience flying solo.

The European leg of that journey proved uneventful, but MacDonald's luck changed once he entered the Middle East. His plane was damaged in an accident while landing in Baghdad. Then, after repairs were completed, he crashed once again, this time in the Sahara Desert. An Arab group took MacDonald into custody, but released him following diplomatic intervention by the Italian military. MacDonald abandoned his planned journey to India and returned home.

Despite the accidents and his limited flying experience, MacDonald began planning for a transatlantic crossing. The success of Lindbergh, combined with patriotism, inspired him to make the perilous journey. MacDonald decided to use a small de Havilland Gypsy Moth biplane, which was the same open-cockpit aircraft he had used the previous year on his unsuccessful voyage to India. The single-engine craft generated eighty-five horsepower, just a fraction of the 220 horsepower produced by Lindbergh's *Spirit of St Louis*. By crossing the Atlantic in the Gypsy Moth, MacDonald planned to set a record for flying the smallest aircraft across the ocean.

MacDonald did not appear to appreciate the dangers of flying across the Atlantic. The plane's open cockpit left him unprotected from the cold autumn weather; but, more critically, he had only half an hour's experience of night flying and had never flown over a huge expanse of ocean with no landmarks to guide him.

In a parting letter to his wife, MacDonald justified his decision to make the journey:

I know you are against the flight. I know that people will say that I am a suicidal fool, but I do not think so. After all, they called Lindbergh "the flying fool". If an American can do it, then so can an Englishman.

In the letter MacDonald also acknowledged that he would possibly never see her or their five-year-old son again, and furthermore, if he died, she should allow their boy to join the army if he were to show an interest. He then apologised to her: "If I have made a mistake, I am sorry. It will be terrible for you."

His plane was sent to Harbour Grace from St John's by train, where it was reassembled for the flight to England. MacDonald took off on October 23 after waiting three weeks for suitable weather. Before leaving, MacDonald confidently predicted that he would meet his wife the next day. He also listed his provisions for the flight:

> I am taking with me a quart thermos bottle of coffee and two dozen sandwiches. I hope to eat the balance of the sandwiches in London tomorrow.

He had difficulty lifting the plane into the air from the airfield because of the heavy load of fuel on board. A Dutch ship, *Hardenburg*, spotted MacDonald's plane about 960 kilometres east of Cape Race, the southeastern tip of Newfoundland. The Gypsy Moth then disappeared. No wreckage was found.

MacDonald's doomed effort would not be the last flight to end in tragedy. In October 1929 the delusions of a Montana cattle rancher led to his lonely demise in the Atlantic Ocean. Urban F Diteman believed that he was a direct descendant of Sir Francis Drake, the sixteenth-century English privateer and vice-admiral who circumnavigated the world in 1580 in a ship named *Golden Hind*. This belief inspired Diteman to emulate his hero by crossing the Atlantic in an aircraft.

Diteman had purchased a small Barling-manufactured single-engine plane in 1928 during a cattle-selling trip in Kansas City, Missouri. Although the aircraft was not designed for long-distance travel, Diteman believed it had the capability of flying non-stop to England from Newfoundland. While privately preparing for a transatlantic flight, Diteman explained, to anybody who asked, that he had acquired the plane for a tour of South America. Prior to departing for Newfoundland from his home in Billings, Montana, he informed friends that he was flying to Saint John, New Brunswick, to conduct genealogical research on his family.

In October 1929, Diteman flew to Roosevelt Field, New York, and from there to Canada, landing in Fredericton, New Brunswick. The airman arrived in St John's on October 16. At Lester's Field, where Alcock and Brown had departed

Above: Harold MacDonald (right), seen
here with Harbour Grace airstrip supervisor
Harold Archibald (centre), suffered the same
fate as many transatlantic aviators during
the 1920s and 1930s and was never seen
again after taking off from Harbour Grace.
Right: Harold MacDonald preparing for his
transatlantic flight.

89

Another solo flyer, American Urban Diteman, greatly underestimated the perils of flying across the Atlantic Ocean. He and the Golden Hind, *which was named after one of the ships commanded by sixteenth-century English adventurer, Sir Francis Drake, disappeared.*

for Ireland in 1919, Mayor Tasker Cook attended the christening of Diteman's plane, which he named *Golden Hind*.

Prior to leaving Newfoundland for England, Diteman wrote a letter that offered a glimpse into his fragile mental state:

Drake did not bring me here nor to London — albeit I am a descendant. Sorry if I hurt any one's feelings and I meant no harm.

Dite

P.S. Many thanks, you will hear from me.

After spending three days in St John's, Diteman flew to Harbour Grace. He took off for England on October 22, and was never seen again.

Eight months later, in June 1930, the dense fog that frequently blankets much of the Northwest Atlantic almost claimed the life of Australia's greatest flying hero, Charles Kingsford-Smith, who was completing a round-the-world flight. If not for the experience and caution of Kingsford-Smith and his crew, the *Southern Cross* would have disappeared — as so many others had — flying west across the North Atlantic.

By this time only the *Bremen* had completed an east-to-west crossing of the Atlantic, and this effort could only have be termed a partial success since it had ended in a crash-landing on Greenly Island.

Two years after the *Bremen* crash, Kingsford-Smith decided to succeed where the German flight had failed, by achieving the first non-stop flight to New York from Europe.

Kingsford-Smith, who had spent four years of his childhood on Canada's west coast, in Vancouver, British Columbia, flew fighter planes for Australia during the First World War. After the war he earned a living my attending air shows and working as a Hollywood stunt pilot. By 1930, Kingsford-Smith was already well known for his endurance flights. In 1928, he and a crew of three had achieved the first flight across the Pacific, from California to Australia, with refuelling stops in Hawaii and Fiji. The Pacific crossing was made in the *Southern Cross*, a three-engine Fokker-built aircraft. Kingsford-Smith followed this achievement with the first non-stop flight across Australia.

By 1930, Kingsford-Smith was ready to attempt a round-the-world flight, and in May the *Southern Cross* took off from Oakland, California. The plane flew westward across the Pacific and reached Baldonnel Airfield in Dublin, Ireland,

after three weeks of travel.

For the dangerous Atlantic crossing Kingsford-Smith selected as his crew professionals who were familiar with flying in poor weather conditions over the world's oceans. Joining him were Dutch KLM pilot Evert van Dyk, navigator Jonathon Saul of Ireland, and New Zealand radio operator John Stannage.

The Irish government went to extraordinary lengths to assist the *Southern Cross*. It ordered 500 soldiers from the Curragh Camp military training centre to prepare a makeshift airstrip on a beach at Portmarnock, a community northeast of Dublin.

Additional fuel tanks were installed inside the cabin of the plane, providing enough gasoline to last thirty-five hours of flying. The plane was flown to Portmarnock, where it waited for almost three weeks for weather to clear over the North Atlantic.

Before leaving Ireland on the Atlantic crossing, Kingsford-Smith was presented with a golden shamrock, for luck. As events unfolded, it became apparent that the *Southern Cross* and its crew would need all the luck — and extra gasoline — they could muster.

The plane finally took off on June 23. For provisions, each man was given a thermos of coffee; ham, egg, and tomato sandwiches; and malted milk tablets.

The plane made steady progress until nightfall, when it encountered a massive fog bank. Kingsford-Smith and van Dyk tried to escape it by climbing and descending, but to no avail. When the radio ceased working, and then blinked back on, Kingsford-Smith surmised it happened because the antenna — located on the underside of the plane — had struck the ocean waves.

Despite carrying a radio, the flyers were unable to get their bearings, since navigation still relied heavily upon visual cues from the stars, moon, and sun. The *Southern Cross* was speeding blindly through the night. The crew became increasingly frustrated, especially with the lack of communication from Newfoundland's Cape Race radio station. Kingsford-Smith's log entry at 11:02 p.m. on June 24 reads:

Poor weather conditions forced one of Australia's greatest aviators to pay an unexpected call on Harbour Grace (opposite and below) during a round-the-world voyage by the Southern Cross *in 1930. Charles Kingsford-Smith (opposite centre) flew his Fokker F-VIIb on several record-breaking flights, until his death in 1935.*

> We're within 100 miles [160 kilometres] of Cape Race, but the big stiff doesn't reply.

It was later estimated that the *Southern Cross* was, in fact, at least 240 kilometres away at the time. Fatigue also became a hazard, as another log entry shows:

> Dickens of a struggle to stay awake now. Drone makes you tired.

As dawn broke, the Cape Race and Belle Isle radio stations were able to guide the plane towards Harbour Grace. By now the men were becoming desperate, and Kingsford-Smith pleaded for a plane to be sent that could guide them through the fog to the airstrip.

No help came. Eventually, however, a hole appeared in the fog over Harbour Grace and the *Southern Cross* was finally able to land after being airborne for over thirty-one hours. Even though the Harbour Grace stop was unplanned, the *Southern Cross* had become the first aircraft to arrive safely in North America after flying the treacherous east-west route across the Atlantic.

They left Harbour Grace the next day and landed at Roosevelt Field, Long Island, a few hours later. Unfortunately, Kingsford-Smith had failed to achieve his goal of flying non-stop from Europe to New York, a mark that would elude aviators until 1932. The *Southern Cross* then embarked on an air tour of the United States before completing its round-the-world journey at Oakland on July 4 – Independence Day.

Like many of the early aviators, Kingsford-Smith died in an air accident; he disappeared over the Bay of Bengal in 1935 when his aircraft flew into a typhoon.

While Kingsford-Smith was preparing for his transatlantic flight in Ireland, Dublin's Baldonnel Airfield had hosted another flyer who was busy rethinking his decision to fly the dangerous westward route across the ocean.

Charles Sanford Wynne-Eyton had won Britain's Distinguished Service Order as a pilot during the First World War and continued to serve with the Royal Air Force until 1926. He then found work in Rhodesia, where he ran a tobacco plantation.

In June 1930, he arrived in Dublin with his small, single-engine Puss Moth monoplane, built by Britain's de Havilland Aircraft Company, which he planned to fly to Newfoundland. The plane, which had been modified by adding fuel tanks, was nicknamed "the flying gas tank", and Wynne-Eyton claimed that this extra fuel capacity would give the plane a range of 4,800 kilometres. He planned to release one of the tanks, which was situated underneath the plane, in flight once it had been emptied.

After assessing the risks of flying westward across the Atlantic, Wynne-Eyton decided to complete the less risky Newfoundland-to-Ireland route instead. He crated the plane and travelled by ship to St John's. From St John's he planned to fly to Harbour Grace, and from there to Europe.

On July 6 Wynne-Eyton took off from Lester's Field in St John's, bound for Harbour Grace. But disaster struck as the plane left the airstrip, when its engine stalled only twelve metres from the ground. The Puss Moth dived, bursting into flames as it crashed to earth. Spectators rushed to the burning wreck and managed to pull its unconscious pilot from the cockpit. Wynne-Eyton survived, but spent several weeks in hospital recovering from severe burns. He returned home and never attempted another transatlantic flight. Wynne-Eyton flew aircraft for Britain during the Second World War. He was killed in an air crash in northern France in 1944.

Show business melded easily with aviation in the post-First World War years, an era when record-setting pilots could expect tickertape parades in New York City and enthusiastic crowds treated them like conquering heroes during victory tours of North America and Europe. Ruth Elder had used her unsuccessful transatlantic flight to land acting roles in feature films, while others, such as Lindbergh, Earhart, and Byrd, established lucrative careers as aviators due to their exploits.

It was therefore fitting that a Broadway producer would play a prominent role in the glamorous world of long-distance aviation. In addition to being an acclaimed member of New York's theatrical fraternity, John Mears had previously set records for travelling around the world.

In 1913, Mears circled the globe in thirty-five days by ship, train, and flying boat. His record stood for thirteen years, until broken in 1926 by Linton Wells and Edward Evans. Like Mears, Wells and Evans used several modes of transportation.

In 1928, Mears was determined to set the record once again, so he hired pilot

Charles Collyer to fly a Fairchild-made FC-2W monoplane, named *City of New York*, on a highly publicised voyage around the world. The global trip, dubbed "Racing the Moon" by Mears, was supposed to be completed within twenty-seven days, the time it takes for the moon to orbit the earth. The two men, and a dog named Tailwind, succeeded, and circled the world in a record-setting twenty-three days. Although impressive for the time, Mears and Collyer did not travel entirely by plane – to cross the Atlantic Ocean, they had boarded a ship.

Two years later, in 1930, Mears decided to circumnavigate the world entirely by plane, and to beat the time of twenty-one days set in 1929 by an airship, the *Graf Zeppelin*. He purchased a Lockheed Vega and again named it *City of New York*. The Vega, like the Fairchild used in 1928, was christened by the wife of New York City's mayor, Jimmy Walker.

Mears needed a new dog as mascot for the journey because Tailwind had been killed by a hit-and-run driver in 1929. No ordinary dog would do, however, and Mears successfully appealed to Canadian-born screen actress Mary Pickford, who gave him her dog, which he named Tailwind II. Numerous delays compelled Mears's pilot to resign, but the *City of New York* finally departed Roosevelt Field on August 2, 1930, with a replacement pilot, Henry Brown.

"Sandy" Wynne-Eyton almost died when his de Havilland Puss Moth (left and above) caught fire while taking off from St John's.

The plane landed at Harbour Grace after an eight-hour flight. Early next morning, Mears and Brown prepared for takeoff in the darkness using flares and lights to guide the *City of New York* down the airstrip. As the plane gained speed, however, its wheels struck a rock, causing it to career off the runway and into the brush. The men escaped unharmed, but the plane was extensively damaged.

During the confusion that surrounded the accident, Pickford's dog disappeared. Mears darkly surmised that a local resident had kidnapped Tailwind II, and he offered a reward for the dog's return. The animal was recovered two days after the accident, filthy, hungry, and drenched by rain — in its fright the dog had simply run away. Mears returned to New York, and he made no further attempts at flying around the world.

Two months after Mears's accident, Harbour Grace hosted the man who became Canada's first transatlantic flying hero. Erroll Boyd was an unlikely candidate to set the Canadian record because the Toronto native had been denied entry as a member of Britain's new Royal Flying Corps during the initial months of the First World War, due to colour-blindness. Persistence paid off, however, as the Royal Naval Air Service, which used a different visual test, accepted Boyd as a pilot. He was taught to fly by John Alcock, who would later make the first

An attempted round-the-world voyage by John Mears (left and below) ended soon after arriving in Harbour Grace from Roosevelt Field, Long Island. The aircraft crashed during takeoff and was damaged beyond repair.

non-stop transatlantic flight with Arthur Whitten Brown.

In 1915, Boyd's wartime activities came to an abrupt end, as his aircraft was shot down over the Netherlands, which was then neutral. Although he was officially designated a prisoner of war, Boyd was allowed to travel freely within the country and was even permitted visits to the United States — which was also neutral until 1917 — on medical grounds.

While in New York he married a Broadway dancer, Evelyn Carberry, whom he had met in Toronto prior to the war. Through her he met singer Al Jolson and other entertainers, encounters that inspired Boyd to put his talents as a songwriter to use. He wrote several popular songs, one of which became a hit on Broadway after the war. Despite his wartime success as a songwriter and a pilot, neither occupation earned Boyd a steady income; during the immediate post-war years he worked at a variety of jobs, including at a car rental agency and managing a hotel.

In the mid-1920s, he obtained employment as a charter and airmail pilot and gained considerable experience flying long distances and coping with harsh weather conditions. After being hired by Charles Levine's Columbia Aircraft Company in 1929, Boyd and navigator Harry Connor flew the *Columbia* on a record-breaking non-stop return flight between New York and Bermuda in June 1930. This was the same aircraft that Levine and Clarence Chamberlin had flown across the Atlantic three years earlier. In 1928, Mabel Boll flew the *Columbia* to Newfoundland on her aborted bid to become the first woman to fly across the Atlantic.

Connor's navigational skills so impressed Boyd during their Bermuda flight that he invited the American to accompany him on his transatlantic flight later in 1930. But first, Boyd needed to get the *Columbia* to Harbour Grace — this turned into a trial equivalent in difficulty to the transatlantic flight itself. With little money of his own, Boyd relied upon sponsors to finance the project; during the Great Depression such support was not readily available.

Finding no backers in Toronto, Boyd sought help in Montreal. However, upon landing at St Hubert Airport on September 1, he was met by members of the Royal Canadian Mounted Police. Officers impounded the plane — which Boyd had renamed the *Maple Leaf* — on behalf of one of Levine's creditors. Although he succeeded in finding financial support for the transatlantic flight, Boyd's hotel bills remained unpaid and continued to mount as the days passed.

A court finally released the plane after almost two weeks, but by then neither Boyd nor Connor had any money to pay the hotel. Rather than wait for a benefactor, the two men snuck out of the building, raced to the airport, and flew their plane to Prince Edward Island. A brewery eventually paid the aviators' Montreal hotel charges, and on September 23, after ten days on Prince Edward

Island, the *Maple Leaf* finally took off and landed in Harbour Grace.

By this time autumn had set in, and with it the onset of unpredictable weather. Although nobody had successfully crossed the Atlantic so late in the year, Boyd and Connor decided to proceed with their flight to Croydon Airport in London.

On October 9, after waiting over two weeks for favourable weather, Boyd and Connor took off from Harbour Grace. Like the *City of New York* a few months earlier, the *Maple Leaf* almost ended its journey in a heap of tangled metal — it skidded along the airstrip and came close to flipping over. Once the plane was airborne, the airmen then battled strong winds, and at higher altitudes ice built up on the wings.

Their closest brush with danger occurred the next day as the *Maple Leaf* neared Europe; a clogged line was preventing them from using fuel in the reserve tank. With almost no usable fuel remaining, Boyd and Connor searched the horizon for land. Fortunately, luck was with them, as they soon came upon the Isles of Scilly, a group of islands forty-five kilometres southwest of Land's End, the western-most point in mainland England. Boyd landed the *Maple Leaf* at a beach on the island of Tresco, which had been used by Britain during the First World War as a seaplane base.

With this achievement, the *Maple Leaf* became the first plane to fly across the

Atlantic outside the summer months, and Boyd the first Canadian to complete a transatlantic flight. The aircraft had also become the first to cross the Atlantic twice, the first time being in 1927 when it was named *Columbia*.

Both Boyd and Connor continued flying throughout the 1930s, with Boyd working as an aviation columnist with the *Toronto Star Weekly*. During the Second World War, Boyd moved to the United States where he recruited pilots for Canada and Great Britain. In 1938, millionaire Howard Hughes hired Connor to navigate his plane on what became a record-setting round-the-world flight.

Opposite: Erroll Boyd (left) became the first Canadian to complete a transatlantic flight. His navigator was an American, Harry Connor (right). Below: Columbia *was renamed* Maple Leaf *by Erroll Boyd for his transatlantic flight. It set out from Harbour Grace on October 9, 1930.*

Wolfgang von Gronau's Dornier Wal *flew across the Atlantic from Germany to Cartwright via Greenland.*

CHAPTER 5

FLYING THE ARCTIC ROUTE

As the number of deaths and accidents among Atlantic flyers mounted during the late 1920s, many aviators sought alternate routes in order to avoid the foggy skies that frequently blanket the ocean east of Newfoundland. Charles Lindbergh had mused about converting aging freighters into permanent refuelling bases at sea. However, although the United States Navy was building its first fleet of aircraft carriers at the time, the costs of maintaining similar ships for civilian or commercial use made Lindbergh's idea impractical.

The most obvious alternative was to avoid the most dangerous area of the North Atlantic altogether, by flying over the Arctic. Under this proposal, new routes would be charted for the coming age of commercial airliners, with planes

The crew of a German seaplane, led by pilot Wolfgang von Gronau, paid a visit to the Labrador community of Cartwright in 1930 (above) after crossing the Atlantic from Europe.

crossing over Greenland and Canada's far north. In 1926, Roald Amundsen had already flown an airship over the North Pole, to Alaska from the Norwegian island of Spitsbergen. For two men, Parker Dresser Cramer of the United States and Wolfgang von Gronau of Germany, Amundsen's flight suggested the viability of commercial airline routes using the Arctic to link Europe with North America.

Cramer, whose uncle established the Dresser manufacturing firm, would make three attempts at flying over the Far North to Europe, using Chicago as his starting point for his first two bids. In his first flight, in 1928, Cramer and another airman, Bert Hassell, embarked on a flight from Illinois to Stockholm, Sweden. During the journey they became lost while flying over Greenland. As the plane ran out of fuel, Cramer was forced to land on Frederikshåb Glacier in southwestern Greenland, several hundred kilometres off course.

Carrying a gun and some food, the men hiked towards a meteorological station, which they thought could be reached in two days. They seriously miscalculated; after walking for fifteen days across Greenland Cramer and Hassell were finally rescued by an Inuit hunter.

A year later, in July 1929, Cramer made a second attempt, this time with the support of Robert McCormick, the eccentric publisher of the Chicago *Tribune* newspaper. McCormick had created a sensation in journalism by ordering his reporters to abandon traditional spelling and to write phonetically — a grammatical innovation he soon abandoned.

McCormick owned two Sikorsky S-38 amphibious aircraft, one of which was named *Untin Bowler*, a slang term for a type of English hunting cap. On July 3 Cramer, along with co-pilot Robert Gast and *Tribune* aviation editor Robert Wood, took off from Chicago in the *Untin Bowler*. They planned to fly over the Arctic and land in Berlin;

An attempt by Parker Cramer (right) to reach Europe by crossing over the Arctic ended prematurely when pack ice crushed his plane at Port Burwell (above), on Killinek Island at the northernmost tip of Labrador, in 1929.

the flyers would then turn around and travel the same route back to Chicago. However, poor weather compelled them to take a much longer tour of Canada's Far North than anticipated. They spent five days battling strong winds and dense fog, and were forced to refuel at isolated government outposts along James Bay.

Their goal was to land at the Royal Canadian Mounted Police outpost of Port Burwell, located near Cape Chidley on Killinek Island at the northernmost tip of Labrador, before heading east across the Greenland ice cap. The radio operator at Port Burwell would end up playing a critical role in guiding the *Untin Bowler* across Canada's North. Throughout the journey, Wood transmitted news articles from the plane back to the *Tribune* in Chicago. His reports illustrated the difficulties faced by Cramer and Gast:

> Fog lay in about the hills as the *Bowler* flew northward. We caught the first sight of the lofty Labrador mountains to the east. Cape Chidley and the whole northern point of Labrador was blanketed in fog, with only the tops of the mountains and hills visible.

In another report Wood described the isolation and rugged beauty of Ungava Bay:

> It is a veritable "no man's land" of muskeg swamps, rock, and stunted forests. Of government patrols in this territory there are none — no fire rangers and no forest fire protective planes, for it is all beyond the limit of marketable timber growth, and stunted birch, balsam fir, black and white spruce, and larch, dot the landscape.

On July 9, the *Untin Bowler* finally landed at Amittoq Inlet near Port Burwell. Local Inuit men were hired to carry drums of fuel to the aircraft, but poor weather repeatedly prevented it from taking off. Worse yet, sea ice began moving into the inlet. The plane taxied into nearby Fox Harbour, where it was moored beneath an abandoned Moravian mission church. Still, slabs of ice threatened the *Untin Bowler*. The crew and volunteers managed to push ice away several times, but on July 12 nature finally prevailed, and they could only watch as the plane crumpled and sank beneath a large slab of ice. The trio was forced to remain at Port Burwell until a supply ship arrived at the end of July.

Cramer's two initial failed attempts did not dissuade a German aviator, Wolfgang von Gronau, who also believed that it was safer and more economically feasible to establish commercial routes over the Arctic than to fly across the Atlantic. Despite being one of Germany's most influential airmen, Gronau had trouble convincing government authorities about the merits of using flying boats to carry mail and passengers along his proposed Greenland route.

The son of an army general, Gronau had flown seaplanes during the First World War. He became a director of a government-financed flying school in the mid-1920s, teaching students to operate small float planes and larger flying boats. To train his students, Gronau often flew with them to Iceland in a German-made Dornier *Wal* flying boat. This aircraft had been flown by Roald Amundsen in an unsuccessful attempt at crossing the North Pole in 1925.

On August 18, 1930, the *Wal* — German for whale — took off from the port of List on the North Sea for what Gronau said was a routine flight from Germany to Iceland. In fact, he intended to fly to New York City. Gronau was highly secretive about his plans: "I did not want blame attached to my name as a pilot if originally announced plans were not carried out successfully," explained Gronau, who did not even confide in his wife.

Accompanying Gronau was co-pilot Edouard Zimmer, a recent graduate of the flying school, as well as mechanic Franz Hack and radio operator Fritz Albrecht. The *Wal* completed its journey with relative ease. After refuelling at Iceland and Greenland, the plane arrived in Cartwright, Labrador, on August 23, where the crew stayed overnight. The next day they flew to Halifax, Nova Scotia. On August 26 Gronau and his crew were welcomed by thousands of onlookers as they landed under the Statue of Liberty in New York harbour.

Despite Gronau's success, airlines remained skeptical about flying the so-called Greenland route. So in August 1931 both Gronau and Cramer decided to fly once again across the Arctic and northern Europe. Cramer — who was now embarking on his third attempt — took off first, leaving Detroit with the

Von Gronau and three crewmen flew a Dornier Wal from Germany to Cartwright to test the viability of using northern routes across the Atlantic Ocean. The seaplane flew on to Quebec, Western Canada,
and the United States.

Opposite: Enthusiasm for Parker Cramer's attempt at reaching Europe by flying over the Arctic
was reflected in media coverage, including this lighthearted cartoon in the Chicago Tribune.

goal of landing in Copenhagen, Denmark. For a while it appeared that Cramer
would finally succeed, since he and navigator Oliver Paquette flew over northern Canada and Greenland without incident and landed safely at the Shetland
Islands. But after taking off on August 9 for the last leg of their trip, their aircraft disappeared as it came within sight of Norway.

A month later, wreckage from the plane was found in the North Sea, and
five months after the crash Cramer's briefcase containing letters and maps were
found by the crew of a fishing boat near the Norwegian city of Stavanger.

A further blow to Arctic flight came from Gronau, whose experiences flying over Greenland proved so harrowing that he changed his mind about the viability of the northern route. Less than a week after Cramer's disappearance, Gronau and his crew arrived safely in Chicago, following a flight from Germany. However, it proved to be a perilous journey as the *Wal* came close to crashing into

A LOT OF ADVENTURESOME YOUTHS LIKE TO STOW'AWAY

Greenland's ice cap. Due to what Gronau said was the "rarified atmosphere" over Greenland and the towering ice fields, the crew had to jettison fuel in order to gain altitude and avoid disaster.

Despite such misgivings, Gronau again flew over Greenland the following year when he completed a round-the-world flight in his aging aircraft. The plane, with co-pilot Geth von Roth, Albrecht, and Hack, left Germany on July 22, 1932. They stopped at Iceland and Greenland, before arriving at Cartwright on July 26. The *Wal* then flew west, touching down at Montreal, Ottawa, Detroit, Chicago, Milwaukee, Winnipeg, Prince Rupert, and three communities in Alaska. The plane proceeded to the Soviet Union, southeast Asia, the Middle East, and Italy. Four months after starting the journey, on November 23, the plane returned to Germany.

Although Gronau had circumnavigated the globe, German authorities remained skeptical about long-distance travel using heavier-than-air machines. The country had become the world's leader in airship technology and craft such as the highly successful *Graf Zeppelin* convinced Germans that these vessels were the only practical way for passengers to fly over the world's oceans. Gronau's dream for a northern route failed to come to fruition, but his career soared after the Nazis took power in 1932. He became president of the German Aero Club, and in 1939 was appointed air attaché to the German embassy in Tokyo.

The failures of Cramer and Gronau had not yet stopped those who believed in using the Arctic to link North America and Europe by air. In July 1933 North American newspapers paid scant notice to the activities of the world's best-known aviator, Charles Lindbergh, when he and his wife, Anne, stepped from their plane at a lake near St John's, Newfoundland, to shake hands with a group of airline representatives and government officials.

Public attention was instead focused on a fleet of Italian seaplanes, led by Italo Balbo, which was in Labrador at the time, en route from Europe to Chicago to celebrate the tenth anniversary of Benito Mussolini's regime. In fact, while the Italians were creating headlines, the Lindberghs and leading members of the

• •

Charles and Anne Lindbergh were greeted by dignitaries upon their arrival at Bay Bulls Big Pond, near St John's. They flew a seaplane named Tingmissartoq, *a Greenland Inuit word meaning "one who flies like a bird".*

• •

airline industry were discussing crucial issues that would eventually result in regular transatlantic passenger flights between Europe and North America.

Pan American World Airways had hired Lindbergh and his wife, Anne Morrow Lindbergh, to determine the viability of using the Greenland route to traverse the Atlantic. In conjunction with a research ship, the *Jellinge*, they would survey possible seaplane landing sites in Newfoundland, Labrador, Greenland, and Iceland.

The timing of the survey was no coincidence — it began at the commencement of an international meeting in St John's involving Pan American, British-based Imperial Airways, and government officials from United States, Great Britain, Canada, and Newfoundland. When deliberations ended two weeks later, the participants had agreed to cooperate on establishing a transatlantic air service. This pact proved to be a significant milestone in the history of flight and would eventually lead to the creation of air service between North America and Europe.

The Lindberghs had begun their journey on July 9, taking off from Long Island in a Lockheed-built Sirius aircraft. The plane was named *Tingmissartoq*, a Greenland Inuit word meaning "one who flies like a bird". With Charles in the pilot seat and Anne as navigator and radio operator, the pair stopped in Maine and Halifax before arriving in Newfoundland on July 12. Their scheduled landing spot was a body of water named Bay Bulls Big Pond, twelve miles south of St John's. Instead they mistakenly landed at the city on Quidi Vidi Lake. A group of surprised onlookers gave the unexpected visitors directions, and within minutes the Lindberghs arrived at their destination.

Pan American's representative at the international meeting, Alan Wilson, greeted the aviators as they stepped ashore. Fêted at a party held in their honour by delegates to the aviation conference, the Lindberghs socialised for only an hour before retiring for the evening. This reluctance to appear at public events would be repeated frequently over the course of their travels over the coming months. Just one year earlier, their son, Charles Jr, had been kidnapped and murdered. In the months and years following this tragedy, the couple would become increasingly reclusive.

On July 14, they took off from St John's and headed west to Botwood, a community in central Newfoundland. Botwood was chosen because it had already been used as a float plane base by a Newfoundland aviator, Sidney Cotton, who began an airmail and aerial survey company in 1921. With Botwood as the base for the Aerial Survey Company, Cotton delivered mail to isolated communities

*In 1932, the kidnapping and murder of
Charles and Anne Lindbergh's
son, Charles Jr, transfixed the
public and led to the most extensive
manhunt in US history. Their twenty-
month-old son was plucked from his crib, with
the kidnapper leaving a ransom note demanding
$50,000 for his safe return. The Lindberghs
paid the ransom, but the boy's badly decomposed
body was later recovered near their New Jersey
estate. Two years later, in 1934, police
arrested a German immigrant, Bruno
Hauptmann. The trial, dubbed by author
HL Mencken as "The greatest story since the
Resurrection", resulted in Hauptmann's convic-
tion. He was executed by electric chair in 1936.*

throughout the island and Labrador.

Although the Lindberghs stayed only a
few hours in Botwood, their visit would
prove pivotal to the future of aviation.
Its deep harbour and location on a great
circle route between Europe and North
America would lead to Botwood becoming a refuelling stop for transatlantic
passenger planes within six years of the
Lindberghs' visit.

Their next stop was Cartwright, in
Labrador, where they had hoped to meet
Balbo and his fleet of seaplanes. But
the Italians had left one day earlier, on
July 13, for New Brunswick, en route to
Chicago. Dense fog then grounded the
Tingmissartoq for almost a week.

While the couple waited in Cartwright,
an agreement was being signed in St
John's that would allow two of the world's
largest airlines to begin commercial
transatlantic air service. Imperial Airways
signed an agreement with the government

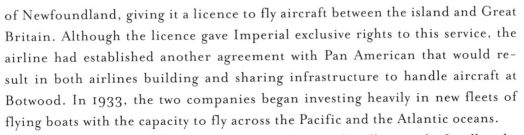

Charles and Anne Lindbergh at Roosevelt Airfield, New York, in December 1929.

of Newfoundland, giving it a licence to fly aircraft between the island and Great Britain. Although the licence gave Imperial exclusive rights to this service, the airline had established another agreement with Pan American that would result in both airlines building and sharing infrastructure to handle aircraft at Botwood. In 1933, the two companies began investing heavily in new fleets of flying boats with the capacity to fly across the Pacific and the Atlantic oceans.

On July 20, the skies finally cleared over Cartwright, allowing the Lindberghs to fly north towards Greenland. They spent a night in the Labrador village of

Hopedale, and then stopped for a few hours at the now-abandoned Moravian missionary community of Hebron, located close to the northernmost tip of Labrador.

The *Tingmissartoq* finally joined the supply ship, *Jellinge,* at Godthaab in western Greenland on July 22, following a six-hour flight from Hebron. A group of Inuit and Danish officials cheered the plane from atop cliffs overlooking the town, and children presented Anne Lindbergh with a bouquet of Greenland poppies as she stepped ashore. At an official reception that evening she told Danish officials:

I shall never forget the majestic beauty of the mountains as we first saw them towering, glistening white, above the clouds. We seemed to be in a new and fantastic world.

During their twenty-four days in Greenland, the Lindberghs surveyed coastal areas of the Danish territory, flying from Canada's Baffin Island to Greenland's east coast. After completing this portion of their work, the Lindberghs flew to Iceland. They finished the Arctic survey at the Faroe Islands in mid-August.

With the formal work now complete, the Lindberghs spent the remainder of the year travelling, ostensibly on vacation. But they could hardly avoid the publicity that followed their every step; huge crowds met them in Denmark, Sweden, Norway, the Soviet Union, Netherlands, France, Spain, and Portugal. In late November, the famous couple travelled to the resort city of Villa Cisneros (re-named Dahkla) in Western Sahara. Two weeks later, they flew across the southern Atlantic, reaching the Brazilian mainland on December 8. Their twenty-one-nation tour ended in Miami, Florida — where Pan American was then head-quartered.

Although the northern air survey would prove invaluable to air transportation during the Second World War, Charles Lindbergh's findings ended the Greenland route as a viable option for commercial seaplane travel. In his report, Lindbergh wrote:

[The survey] left no doubt in my mind about the wisdom of establishing the first air route to Europe by way of Bermuda and the Azores. Ice conditions along a more northern route would prevent operation of flying boats [during the winter] ... we could never give satisfactory service to transatlantic passengers if we had to move our terminal with the seasons.

With the completion of the Lindberghs' mission, few aviators would attempt to fly over Greenland until the outbreak of the Second World War. A notable exception was physician and world traveller, Richard Upjohn Light.

When Light landed his plane at Cartwright, Labrador, on August 23, 1934, he had hoped to tour the medical facilities run by Sir Wilfred Grenfell, a pioneering physician who dedicated his career to building hospitals and improving the health of aboriginal peoples in the territory.

Unfortunately, Labrador's only hospital had been destroyed by fire a few days prior to Light's arrival. He witnessed medical staff constructing makeshift operating tables out of crates left by Italo Balbo's air squadron a year earlier, and attended the funeral for a girl who perished in the blaze.

Light, who had studied neurosurgery under the tutelage of Harvey Cushing, the world's leading expert in the field, had already commenced a promising career as a physician and an instructor in surgery at Yale University. Nevertheless, he was determined to travel around the world. Light had learned to fly in the late 1920s while serving in the US Army Air Corps, and by 1934 he determined that he had built up enough experience as a pilot to fly around the world. Unlike many of his contemporaries, Light was not concerned with breaking records; his goals were to experience other cultures and to tour areas of the planet rarely visited by Americans.

Light and co-pilot Robert Wilson began their world trip at New Haven, Connecticut, on August 20. One of their first stops was Cartwright, which had become an important refuelling stop for planes commencing the Arctic route to

Europe. During his five days in Labrador, Light travelled by boat with a Grenfell Mission doctor to tiny communities along the coast.

After leaving Labrador, Light and Wilson stopped in Greenland and Iceland before arriving in Europe. The aviators reached the Philippines in December, but from there they decided not to risk a dangerous flight across the Pacific Ocean. Instead, they travelled by ship to Vancouver, British Columbia.

Light and Wilson visited Mexico and Cuba, and finished their five-month-long journey at New Haven on January 22, 1935. Two years later, Light would travel once more by air, this time crossing Africa with his first wife, the re-nowned photographer, Mary Meader. In recognition of his explorations, Light was elected as president of the American Geographic Society in 1947.

Dr Richard Upjohn Light visited Labrador during a round-the-world tour in 1934. The Wisconsin native is seen here with his Pitcairne Mailwing aircraft in 1932.

Italy achieved a public relations victory by flying a squadron of aircraft to North America from Europe in 1933. Led by Air Minister Italo Balbo, the planes stopped in the Newfoundland community of Shoal Harbour in August that year.

CHAPTER 6

FASCISM IN THE AIR

Public enthusiasm for aircraft — and the pioneers who set flying records — was reaching its zenith in the early 1930s, just as the Great Depression was sweeping across Europe and North America. Images of brave men and women soaring into the clouds charged the imaginations of people, millions of whom followed the exploits of their heroes in newspapers, on radio broadcasts, and in newsreels at movie theatres.

Such interest did not escape the notice of politicians, from small-town mayors to national leaders, few of whom could resist being photographed with record-setting pilots, in hopes that they might benefit from reflected glory.

More importantly, aviation had become a useful public relations tool for many

nations after the First World War, as governments linked triumph in the skies with national prowess. While the US, France, and Britain were among the leaders in the propaganda battle, the practice was elevated to new levels in the 1930s by Nazi Germany and Italy's fascist regime.

The most successful of these propagandists was Italy's Air Minister, Italo Balbo. As one of Benito Mussolini's most trusted aides, Balbo had been commander-in-chief of the brutal Blackshirt militias that brought the fascists to power in the early 1920s. Balbo was accused of ordering the beatings of communists, socialists, and trade unionists throughout Italy, and he was implicated in the murders of opposition figures.

Opposite: Dictatorships in Italy and Germany eagerly embraced the propaganda value of aviation. Italian president, Benito Mussolini (centre right), ordered a former thug, Italo Balbo (at his side), to make the air force a showpiece of Italian power.

Below: Balbo in Clarenville with John Puddester, a member of the Newfoundland government, at his right. Puddester was later appointed to the Commission of Government that ruled Newfoundland after its parliament was replaced by non-elected officials in 1934.

Despite having no experience as an aviator, Balbo was appointed by Mussolini to a senior position in the air force in 1926. The debonair former bank clerk's leadership skills were readily apparent, and three years later he was appointed Air Minister. Balbo, who by then had earned his wings as a pilot, began reorganizing the air force into a propaganda tool for Mussolini.

The four-continent tour by Francesco de Pinedo in 1927 had already demonstrated the effectiveness of aviation as a force in uniting Italians. To reinforce the supremacy of fascism and Italy's air prowess, Balbo organised a spectacle never before attempted: a mass transatlantic flight by a squadron of aircraft.

On December 17, 1930, Balbo led twelve Savoia-Marchetti flying boats on a journey to Brazil. After taking off from Ortabello, Italy, the squadron spent several weeks in Portuguese Guinea (now Guinea Bissau). All of the aircraft reached Rio de Janiero safely on January 15, 1931.

The flight was a propaganda bonanza. Huge crowds of spectators watched in fascination as the seaplanes roared overhead and landed one after another in the harbour. When Balbo and his men flew back to Italy, a proud populace greeted them as if they were military heroes.

This proved to be a trial run for an even more ambitious project. In 1933, Balbo organised another mass flight across the Atlantic, but this one would involve twice the number of aircraft and require flying across the treacherous waters of the North Atlantic.

The spectacle was timed to coincide with two events: Mussolini's tenth year as president, and the Century of Progress Exposition in Chicago. A highlight of the world fair would be the unveiling, by Balbo, of a monument to Italian explorer Christopher Columbus.

Twenty-five newly manufactured Savoia-Marchetti S-55 flying boats left Ortabello on June 30. The dozens of airmen chosen for the mission had spent several months training to fly in close formation. Each plane carried a four-man crew consisting of a pilot, co-pilot, engineer, and radio operator.

Balbo's squadron landed first at Amsterdam. Tragically, one of the planes struck a dyke while landing, drowning one crewman and damaging the aircraft beyond repair.

Despite the accident, the remaining aircraft flew on to Londonderry, Ireland. On July 5 the airmen took off for their next destination, Iceland. In Reykjavik, the arrival of a hundred Italian military men created a sensation among the populace and Balbo described their welcome as exceptionally warm and inviting. The Italians enjoyed a week touring Iceland, but seemed especially enthralled by the women they encountered on the island. Balbo wrote in his book, *My Air Armada*:

My Atlantic lads, with the chivalry of their race, pay special attention to the Iceland girls, who are indeed very beautiful and charming. A few of the younger officers are inclined to fall seriously in love with some of the fair visitors to the hotel. But Iceland girls, simple and unsophisticated though they look, are too level-headed and calculating to pay serious attention to the romantic blarney of young Italians who have descended among them suddenly like a bolt from the blue, and who will vanish just as suddenly.

Indeed, on July 12, seven days after their arrival, the airmen took off and headed to their first North American stop, the community of Cartwright on the coast of Labrador.

Balbo described the hours spent in the ocean crossing as a period of constant anxiety, punctuated by moments of terror. For much of the journey, the planes were obscured in rain clouds and dense banks of fog. Balbo recalled:

At one point ... there is an absolute black out. We can see nothing but the gleam of the instruments on the dashboard. We have run into a rain cloud and a torrential downpour drives right into our cabin. I relax my grip for a moment to write a note to Pezzani. But at this moment the plane heels. The plane bounces up and down with quick jerky movements. It is like an earthquake in the air, so to speak. I plead guilty to a fleeting spasm of fright.

The fog dissipated as Balbo's squadron reached Labrador, revealing the stark tree-lined coast and a glistening ocean dotted by patches of white pack ice. Balbo described his joy at seeing North America for the first time on his journey, which he celebrated by sending a telegraph message directly to Mussolini:

> A peculiar sense of semi-intoxication sweeps over me. The sea which sparkles beneath the rays of the sun seems to join in our exaltation with its crystalline foam-capped waves. Our Fascist native land may well be proud of its airmen. They have brought honour to the uniform of the blackshirt, which they will wear proudly as they enter America.

The planes were met in Cartwright harbour by the *Alice*, an Italian supply ship sent to Labrador in advance of Balbo and his men. A US seaplane, carrying a large contingent of journalists and photographers, had also arrived in anticipation of the squadron's arrival. However, the modest Labrador community seemed to have been an anticlimax for the Italian aviators after the excitement of crossing the Atlantic. Balbo described Cartwright as:

> ... a few little timber houses set against a rather depressing background of grayish-green vegetation. Thickets of stunted firs dotted among barren crags.

Nevertheless, residents of Cartwright eagerly welcomed their Italian visitors. Many of them volunteered to help with a banquet held in honour of the airmen, while others assisted in refuelling the twenty-four flying boats.

Dorothy Fequet, one of the children who participated in the Cartwright festivities, recalled the events; her recollections were published in the September 1986 edition of *Them Days* magazine:

Dormitories at the Grenfell Mission were requisitioned by the *Alice* officers, to house the arriving aviators. Case after case of Italian wine came from the ship to load the Mission's cellars for a banquet planned for the airmen; this, to the chagrin of the Mission Matron, for cellars had never held anything stronger than soft drinks.

The banquet that night was something. Portraits of Mussolini and General Balbo adorned the walls with the modest portrait of Sir Wilfred Grenfell, the Mission founder. Italian cooks from the *Alice* prepared the food, while Mission waitresses and other volunteers rushed hither and yon, supplying the Italians with food and trying desperately to cope with the mounting flow of dirty dishes and utensils.

I can remember when Balbo's fleet came to Cartwright. Everybody that could was hired to put oil in the planes, and there was two children picked out to meet General Balbo at the Grenfell Mission dormitory. Noel Groves was dressed as an Italian boy — all dressed in Italian clothes — and I was dressed in Italian girl's clothes. We greeted him on the dormitory steps, shook hands with him and bowed to him.

The squadron took off the following morning, stopping next at Shediac, New Brunswick, where Canadian government officials greeted Balbo and his men. The next day, July 14, they flew along the St Lawrence River and landed at Montreal.

In Montreal, which at that time was Canada's largest city, an enthusiastic crowd of supporters arrived to meet the airmen. An honour guard of Italian Canadians, wearing the blackshirt uniforms of their fascist heroes, formed a cordon around the officers as they stepped ashore.

Even Balbo seemed overwhelmed by the cheering multitudes. After attending a lengthy ceremony, he

Balbo was accorded a hero's welcome at home after a highly successful propaganda effort in North America.

attempted to get some sleep by retiring to the privacy of his hotel room. It was to no avail. A herd of reporters followed the Italian Air Minister into his suite and refused to leave.

The seaplanes departed Montreal the next morning for Chicago, where thousands of people were waiting for the Italians as the aircraft crossed Lake Michigan and landed adjacent the Century of Progress exhibition grounds.

Massive crowds greeted the adventurers wherever they went in Chicago, and a week later in New York City. Among the numerous official events held in Balbo's honour was a dinner at the White House with President Franklin Roosevelt.

To Balbo, this success seemed to buttress the credibility of Italy's dictatorship. In a telegram to Mussolini he reported that all traces of antipathy towards fascism — which he had experienced in a previous visit to the US — had evaporated. He wrote:

> At the meeting in Madison Square [Garden] a distinct political atmosphere — an atmosphere of passionate Fascism prevails.

Balbo's squadron left New York on July 25 on a return flight to Italy. They stopped at Shediac for the night, and headed to Newfoundland the next day. Their destination was Shoal Harbour, a village in Trinity Bay on the northeast coast of the island. Balbo seemed surprised by the sparse, modest amenities awaiting his men in the community, even though the *Alice* had arrived a week earlier in preparation for the arrival of the air fleet.

Railway carriages had been procured and lined up near the wharf as accommodations for the men, as well as a restaurant car for senior officers. Visitors from several nearby communities, some of whom were camping in tents along the roadside, arrived to greet the Italian planes.

Balbo had expected to leave Newfoundland within five days of arriving. Instead, poor weather kept the Italians waiting for two weeks. With high winds in the forecast for several days, Balbo boarded a train on July 31 and visited St John's.

In Newfoundland's capital, he and his officers were treated to a sumptuous luncheon hosted by Prime Minister Frederick Alderdice. The prime minister toasted Balbo and led a chorus of "For He's a Jolly Good Fellow" in "a lusty, baritone voice". Balbo also paid a visit to two Italian submarines that were docked in St John's harbour.

A highlight of the stopover was attending the opening of a new telegraph station at Cabot Tower, a prominent building on Signal Hill overlooking St John's and the entrance to its harbour. In 1901, from a building adjacent Cabot Tower, Guglielmo Marconi had made a technological breakthrough by receiving the first transatlantic wireless message. Now, more than thirty years later, Balbo was sending a message of greetings from Cabot Tower to the inventor's home in Italy. During his short visit to St John's, Balbo also purchased a pair of sealskin slippers for his infant son, and then returned by train to Shoal Harbour.

Finally, the weather cleared, and in the early hours of August 8 the flying boats took off and headed to the Azores. Fog obscured both the sun and the ocean for much of the journey, as it had weeks earlier when they flew to Labrador. One of the seaplanes crashed while landing in the Azores, but fortunately nobody was injured in the mishap.

The remaining twenty-three aircraft continued to Lisbon, Portugal. On August 12, the squadron returned home, landing on the Tiber River in Rome. As Balbo disembarked from his plane, Mussolini was waiting on shore to meet him. Italy's transatlantic adventurers marched in a parade through Rome, and the king of Italy rewarded Balbo by elevating him to the honourary rank of Air Marshall.

Even though he had become a national hero, Balbo's career as Air Minister came to an abrupt end. Mussolini may have viewed Balbo's popularity as a potential threat to his authority, and in 1934 he appointed the airman as governor of Libya. Here, Balbo coordinated Italy's campaign of modernizing Libyan infrastructure, and oversaw immigration to Italy's "Fourth Shore" by thousands of Italian colonists. However, his attempts at converting Libyan Moslems to fascism proved largely unsuccessful.

Balbo died in June 1940 when his aircraft was shot down over the Libyan port of Tobruk, ironically by anti-aircraft fire from an Italian warship riding at anchor in the harbour. The few remaining legacies of his visit to North America

A Dornier flying boat of the early 1930s proved that the era of large passenger aircraft had not yet arrived. The DO-X, shown in Newfoundland, could carry up to seventy people, but was badly underpowered despite carrying twelve engines. In 1934 the DO-X was placed in a German museum, but it was destroyed in a bombing raid on Berlin in 1945.

include a street in Chicago and an elementary school in Shoal Harbour, both of which bear Balbo's name.

Not all exhibitions of aviation prowess were as successful as Balbo's, as the case of the DO-X flying boat would prove. The limitations of this — the world's first transatlantic passenger aircraft — were not immediately obvious, however. Certainly, those who witnessed the DO-X lumbering across the sky and landing on the ocean surface believed they were witnessing a technological revolution.

This view was shared by executives working for Dornier, the German aircraft manufacturer that launched the first DO-X flying boat in 1929, and which hoped that airlines would soon be clamouring to order replicas of the aircraft.

The DO-X was an impressive looking machine; it was the largest aircraft ever built, and it boasted twelve engines mounted on top of a single forty-eight-metre-long wing. Designed by Claude Dornier, the massive seaplane was the epitome of luxury. Its spacious hull held three decks, which contained sleeping quarters, a bar, parlour rooms, a kitchen, and an 18-metre-long dining salon. But the aircraft's size came at a cost. Although it had a large number of engines, the plane remained underpowered; the DO-X weighed fifty tonnes fully loaded and it consumed 1,500 litres of fuel per hour.

Under the command of Captain Friedrich Christiansen the DO-X was supposed to embark upon its maiden crossing of the Atlantic in November 1930. However, engine troubles forced a three-month postponement soon after it left Germany. Then in February 1931, when it arrived in the Canary Islands, the engines had to be overhauled once again. Finally, in June that year — seven months after leaving Germany — it flew across the South Atlantic and reached the Brazilian island of Fernando Noronha.

Several months later, the DO-X began another flight across the Atlantic, this time flying from New York. On May 20, 1932, with Christiansen at the controls, it headed to the eastern Newfoundland community of Holyrood, but poor weather forced it to land first at the nearby town of Dildo.

The DO-X refuelled and departed Newfoundland on May 22, but the aircraft's chronic unreliability forced Christiansen to land short of Horta in the Azores. It travelled to port under its own power on the ocean surface. Despite the DO-X's problems, enthusiastic crowds greeted the plane as it crossed Europe, stopping in Spain, England, and Germany. By then, however, Dornier had realised that the aircraft's shortcomings made it impractical. Advances in safety and reliability were clearly necessary before commercial transatlantic flight by plane would become feasible.

Christiansen, who had been a pilot in the First World War, enjoyed a revival of his military career under the Nazi regime, which came to power in 1932. He was promoted to the rank of general and led Germany's military administration in the Netherlands during occupation of that country in the Second World War. He was charged with war crimes following Germany's defeat, but was acquitted.

Although Germany failed in its attempts at making flying boats reliable enough to cross the Atlantic Ocean, the country had, since the late 1920s, demonstrated its engineering prowess by building the first airborne ocean liner, the airship.

For a few minutes on October 15, 1928, millions of people in the cities of New York and Washington paused and gazed skyward. Rush-hour traffic ground to a halt — drivers and passengers seemingly hypnotised. Supreme Court judges stopped their deliberations and dashed to their windows.

The giant *Graf Zeppelin* airship had arrived from Germany. At 236 metres in length, the cigar-shaped craft was the largest machine ever built. In Lakehurst, New Jersey, 65,000 spectators greeted the *Graf Zeppelin* as it descended gracefully to a landing. Unlike modern lighter-than-air craft that use helium, an inert gas, to provide lift, the *Graf Zeppelin* and its contemporaries were filled with explosive hydrogen gas.

Poor weather and damage to one of the airship's tail fins had slowed its progress across the Atlantic; this resulted in a four-and-a-half-day crossing of the ocean — about two days longer than anticipated. Passengers reported running out of tobacco, but aside from this annoyance, no significant hardships were endured.

The DO-X at the community of Dildo in Newfoundland.

The voyage was billed by the Zeppelin company as a precursor to regular, scheduled commercial flights between Europe, the US, and South America. Not only was the *Graf Zeppelin* important to the business of aviation, the airship would become an important symbol of German superiority in the field of engineering.

Two weeks after arriving in Lakehurst, the *Graf Zeppelin* began its return cruise to Germany. Unlike the westward flight, which followed a route south of the Azores, on its return the airship flew the shorter distance over the treacherous North Atlantic. The dream of airship travel almost ended in disaster over Newfoundland. A massive storm buffeted the *Graf Zeppelin* so much that it was driven backwards towards a group of islands. Hugo Eckner, who headed the Zeppelin firm and was the most experienced airshipman of his era, described the flight as the worst he had experienced. Eckner, who tried to calm passengers by regularly going to the lounge to feed a pet canary, said:

● ●

The most successful commercial airship, the Graf Zeppelin, *began its transoceanic career in 1928. Despite having an impeccable safety record, it was immediately retired after another German airship, the* Hindenburg, *exploded in 1937.*

● ●

This last trip made me think of God. I never regarded it as a small thing to cross the ocean in an airship, but never until now have I quite realised what it meant. The storm which caught us over Newfoundland tossed us in a tumult which threatened at times to break the ship in two. Now we know where all those pilots lost their lives. It was over Newfoundland.

Residents of communities in Trinity Bay reported catching sight of the *Graf Zeppelin* before the airship disappeared travelling east over the horizon. It took three days for the airship to reach the German port of Friedrichshafen.

Following this return flight, improvements were made to the airship's engines. In 1929 the *Graf Zeppelin* circumnavigated the globe in a record twenty-one days. After this achievement, regular passenger flights commenced in 1930 with the airship carrying people, freight, and mail across the Atlantic.

The demand for passenger berths convinced Zeppelin to build a new fleet of airships. The convenience of this mode of travel was undeniable; flights from Frankfurt, Germany, and Lakehurst took just sixty hours, a fraction of the time taken by passenger ships. Fares had also become more affordable since the *Graf Zeppelin* began carrying passengers in 1928. So in 1936 a new airship, the *Hindenburg*, was launched to meet the burgeoning demand for transatlantic airship travel.

Measuring 245 metres, the length of almost three football fields, the *Hindenburg* was even larger than the *Graf Zepplin*. The design was also innovative; unlike its predecessors, the passenger compartment was partially enclosed within the vessel's hull, an innovation that allowed the airship to carry greater numbers of people. Like the luxurious passenger ships that traversed the world's oceans, the *Hindenburg* boasted lounges, staterooms, and an elegant dining salon. On its maiden voyage, in May 1936, passengers were treated to a piano recital.

The *Hindenburg*, which made ten return trips across the Atlantic in 1936, left a vivid impression with those who witnessed it cruising just 400 metres overhead. Among those who were alarmed by the airship were residents of Colliers, a community on the coast of Conception Bay in Newfoundland. Bridgett Flynn, who had been picking berries when the *Hindenburg* approached, remembered:

> We looked to the skies and were amazed. The Zeppelin was the strangest thing we had ever seen and we thought the world was going to come to an end when it came near.

But by the mid-1930s Germany's airships were no longer just a mode of transportation. With the ascendance of the Nazi Party, under the leadership of Adolf Hitler, the country's fleet of airships became obvious tools for promoting Nazism at home and abroad. Swastikas painted onto the tail fins of both the *Graf Zeppelin* and the *Hindenburg* turned them into gigantic advertisements for Germany's fanatical regime.

In 1936 the two airships were used in a referendum on Nazi leadership; they cruised German cities, dropping party literature. The use of Zeppelin airships for this purpose disgusted Hugo Eckner, president of the company and a well-known opponent of Hitler. When the Nazis took power, German newspapers were initially told to cease using Eckner's name in reports, an order that was quickly rescinded. Eckner had become a highly respected figure in the US, and the German regime was loath to risk a new agreement between Zeppelin and the Goodyear company that promised to help the airship industry in both countries.

But political pressures – in combination with business decisions by Zeppelin – had already compromised the safety of passengers who were flying in Germany's airships. Beginning in 1927, the US government banned the export of helium in order to guarantee supplies for its own airships. Helium is inherently safer than hydrogen because it is inert and therefore cannot ignite; however, unlike hydrogen, which can be easily produced, much of the world's helium is extracted from natural gas. Not all natural gas reservoirs contain helium, however, and the US held a virtual worldwide monopoly on the gas prior to the Second World War. Although Zeppelin lobbied the US government to gain access to helium, the company also had its own economic reasons for favouring hydrogen. Not only was helium more expensive, it is also a far heavier gas than hydrogen – and therefore a less effective medium for providing lift.

The aging *Graf Zeppelin* was scheduled for retirement after completing the 1937 season. Between 1928 and 1937 it had flown 1.6 million kilometres without incident, a record of success that greatly reinforced public confidence in airships. From the time it had gone into service, the *Graf Zeppelin* had become the world's most successful airship; its 590 flights included 143 ocean crossings, mostly between Europe and South America.

Despite its unblemished safety record, the *Graf Zeppelin*'s service life came to a premature end, due to one of the most spectacular accidents of the twentieth

Like today's cruise ships, the Hindenburg *was a luxury vessel, and boasted a piano bar and white tablecloth dining.*

century. On May 6, 1937, the *Hindenburg* slowly approached its docking tower at Lakehurst, New Jersey, as it completed its first transatlantic flight of the year. US Navy sailors waited on the ground while mooring ropes were dropped to them from the mammoth airship.

Suddenly, a spark erupted without warning from the stern of the airship. Within seconds, an explosion and sheets of flame ripped into the evening sky. The tanks of hydrogen that had kept the *Hindenburg* aloft during its flight across the Atlantic ignited in rapid succession before an onslaught of searing heat.

The ground crew sprinted to escape the doomed airship as it plunged earthward. Terrified passengers smashed windows and leaped from the gondolas, while families waiting to greet them gasped in horror. Within minutes, a showpiece of the Nazi regime had been reduced to a tangle of blackened, twisted metal.

One passenger, Carl Otto Clemens, described how quickly the mood changed in the main cabin, from quiet anticipation to outright terror:

> I was in the centre of the ship, photographing, when I suddenly saw flames. I ran down a short flight of stairs, not knowing whether to jump or remain aboard. I guess it was only fifteen feet above the ground when I decided to jump. All I can remember is voices screaming.

Thirty-five people died in the disaster, including the captain, Ernst Lehmann. But these were not the only casualties — the *Hindenburg*'s fate also terminated the era of passenger airships, perhaps forever. The accident occurred just as the United States and Germany had been planning the construction of several new airships. These investments were being considered despite the loss of several such vessels to accidents during the previous decade.

Fatal accidents included the *Italia*, an Italian-built craft, which broke apart over Norway during a scientific expedition in 1928, killing several men. British airships, including the *R-100*, which attracted hundreds of thousands of visitors in eastern Canada and the US following a transatlantic voyage in July and August 1930, were permanently grounded two months later when a sister ship, the *R-101*, crashed during its maiden voyage over France. Bound for Karachi, the accident resulted in the deaths of all but six of its fifty-four passengers and crew.

The US had also experienced disasters involving Navy airships, starting with the *Shenandoah*, which broke apart over Ohio in 1925. Then, in 1933, only three of seventy-six people survived when the *Akron* plunged into the ocean near Atlantic City, New Jersey. Similarly, high winds tore the *Macon* to shreds two years later, killing two people. In contrast, until the *Hindenburg* disaster Germany had not recorded any serious accidents involving passenger airships built and operated by the Zeppelin firm since the end of the First World War.

Germany did not immediately terminate its airship program following the *Hindenburg* explosion. The government intensified its efforts at obtaining helium in order to provide lift for a new airship that had been set to enter the transatlantic service. But with a war looming in Europe, the US government had become suspicious about German motives and the moratorium on helium exports remained in place.

In June 1937 the *Graf Zeppelin* was deflated and placed in a hangar, one month after the spectacular destruction of the *Hindenburg*. With the outbreak of war in 1939, the skeleton of the *Graf Zeppelin* was dismantled and melted down to manufacture weapons.

Passenger airships would no longer cruise the world's skies. They would be replaced after the Second World War by a new generation of airliners — which proved to be faster, safer, and more economical to operate.

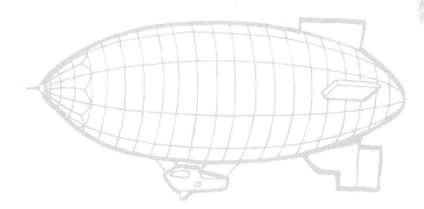

The Hindenburg *exploded without warning while approaching a docking tower at Lakehurst, New Jersey, on May 6, 1937. US Navy sailors, preparing to grab tether lines on the ground, ran for safety as the airship descended in flames.*

CHAPTER 7
FROM BROADWAY TO LONDON AND BACK

Harbour Grace hosted two teams of transatlantic flyers concurrently in June 1930. The Winnie Mae (left) succeeded in flying around the world, while the Liberty (right) flew non-stop to Copenhagen, Denmark.

By the onset of the Great Depression Newfoundland had become the most important link in the chain joining North America and Europe by air, and on this island the main departure and arrival point for transatlantic aircraft was the fishing community of Harbour Grace. The town, located on Newfoundland's northeast coast, boasted an airstrip and a rail line to the city of St John's, which gave it logistical advantages over other centres on the island.

Still, Harbour Grace was not regularly abuzz with the sound of aircraft motors, so considerable excitement was generated in June 1931 when two Europe-bound aircraft took off on the same day — an unprecedented event for any community during the early days of long-distance aviation.

A monoplane, named *Liberty* and built by the American Bellanca Aircraft Company, departed Floyd Bennett Field in Brooklyn on June 22, and arrived in Harbour Grace later that day. Its two crewmen were hoping to complete the first non-stop flight to Copenhagen, Denmark, from North America.

The pilot, Holger Hoiriis, was a native of Denmark who had immigrated to the US following the First World War. Accompanying Hoiriis was a passenger, the plane's owner, Otto Hillig, a German immigrant who became a wealthy portrait photographer in New York State. Hillig had named the plane after Liberty, New York, the city that became his home.

According to newspaper reports, Hillig had purchased his plane using the proceeds from an out-of-court settlement reached with operators of the *Graf Zeppelin* airship in 1928. He had filed a lawsuit against the company when his reservation on a transatlantic flight was cancelled without warning.

On June 24, almost two days after the *Liberty* had landed at Harbour Grace, it was joined by a second plane, the *Winnie Mae*, which had departed from Roosevelt Field, Long Island. But pilots Wiley Post and Howard Gatty had even a grander ambition for the *Winnie Mae* than Hoiriis and Hillig: they were planning to fly around the world, and to break the record of twenty-one days that had been established in 1929 by the *Graf Zeppelin*.

This round-the-world flight would establish the then little-known Post as one of aviation's greatest pioneers. But Post, born part-Cherokee Indian, was perhaps an unlikely candidate to achieve greatness. In his youth Post had served time in jail for stealing a car, and later found work in the Oklahoma oil fields, where he lost an eye in an industrial accident. But this mishap had one benefit: Post was able to use the proceeds from a financial settlement from his employer to buy an aircraft and pursue his love for flying.

In the mid-1920s, Post became the personal pilot of Oklahoma oil tycoon, FC Hall, who in 1930 bought a Lockheed Vega and named it *Winnie Mae*. The Vega model had become popular with many pilots, among them Amelia Earhart, who made several record flights with her machine. Hall agreed to finance Post's dream of flying around the world and hired Gatty, an Australian, as co-pilot.

Although the *Winnie Mae* had started its 1931 journey after the *Liberty*, Post and Garry were determined to beat their rival in crossing the Atlantic. Upon arriving safely in Harbour Grace, they quickly refuelled the plane and took off just four hours later. The Atlantic proved to be the most dangerous part of the world flight for Post and Gatty. Soon after taking off from Harbour Grace, the *Winnie*

Mae was battling the same weather conditions that had plagued many transatlantic aviators. Post recalled:

> There is one thing I don't want to do right away again, and that is to fly the Atlantic. For three hours I could not see the engine at all and I just had to keep my eyes glued to the instruments. And it was only by the grace of God that we found that hole over Bangor in Wales, came down and found out where we were.

The *Winnie Mae* then stopped in England and Germany, before flying for several days over the vast Siberian wilderness. Post said the highlight of his world journey occurred at Irkustk in central Siberia, where most of the city's inhabitants converged to meet the plane. The only English speaker was a sixteen-year-old girl, who did her best to translate. Post wrote:

> The poor girl had spoken no English for six years ... and mixed a strong cockney accent with Russian at first, but gradually we got to understanding each other better and we talked about the various countries we had visited and had a good chat.

On June 30, they reached Fairbanks, Alaska, and on the same day flew 2,330 kilometres to Edmonton, Alberta. Here the *Winnie Mae* was greeted by an enthusiastic crowd of 2,000 people, many of whom broke through a police line to greet the flyers. The plane had landed at Blatchford Field, the first publicly licensed airfield in Canada — later to be renamed Edmonton City Centre Airport. The rain had turned the airstrip into mud, so next morning the *Winnie Mae* was towed to the city's main road, where it took off and headed east.

On July 1, Post and Gatty arrived where they had started, at Roosevelt Field.

They had flown around the world in eight days and sixteen hours, easily smashing the *Graf Zeppelin's* time of twenty-one days and five hours.

Although the *Liberty* had lost the transatlantic race to the *Winnie Mae*, Hoiriis and Hillig were determined to complete their non-stop flight to Copenhagen. They departed Harbour Grace before sunrise on June 24 and soon met one of the greatest hazards to aviation — fog. However, unlike many aviators who had attempted to fly across the Atlantic, Hoiriis had prepared for this particular challenge: in the weeks prior to the flight he had trained himself for flying in fog by covering the windows of the *Liberty* with paper and flying by instrumentation alone. Such precautions, often omitted by other flyers prior to attempting transatlantic crossings, almost certainly saved his and Hillig's lives.

Although Hoiriis's training provided him with the skills necessary to keep the plane from crashing into the ocean and veering wildly off course, he was unable to determine with precision the plane's location. For fifteen hours the *Liberty* flew blind and against strong winds. Eventually, however, the skies opened. Hillig recounted:

> We finally discovered a hole in the clouds which had kept us for what seemed an eternity completely secluded from the world. The changed situation, however, brought no relaxation, since we had not the remotest idea where we were and hardly any way to find out.

The men flew along the coast of northern Europe for several hours, until they finally found an airport, at Krefeld in Germany's Rhineland district. They were too tired to continue further, so they landed and waited until the next day

to fly the remaining 320 kilometres to Denmark. As they arrived in Copenhagen Hoiriis and Hillig were mobbed by 50,000 cheering spectators.

Two years after the *Winnie Mae* set the round-the-world mark, Post decided to lower his record again — but this time he would to do it flying solo. He took off from Floyd Bennett Field, New York, in July 1933 to begin his

Opposite: A radio reporter (kneeling) records a meeting of pioneer airmen in Harbour Grace, as Holger Hoiriis (centre right) shakes Howard Gatty's hand. Between them is Post, with Otto Hillig (in an aviator hat). Top: Humorist and actor Will Rogers, starring in the 1929 film, They Had to See Paris. Above: Upon their arrival back in the United States, Gatty and Post were accorded a tickertape parade along the heart of New York's financial district in July 1931.

quest. This time Post had taken advantage of recent technical advancements by installing an autopilot and radio compass inside the aircraft. He saved time by flying directly from New York to Berlin, but subsequently lost many hours due to equipment malfunctions, minor accidents, and then lost his way over Alaska. On July 22 he once again refuelled the *Winnie Mae* in Edmonton and continued on to New York. Despite the delays, Post had circled the globe in a record time of seven days and nineteen hours.

Post then focused on high-altitude flight, and, in partnership with the BF Goodrich company, he designed a pressurised aviator suit. Post wore one when he took the *Winnie Mae* to an altitude of 15.2 kilometres, reaching the sub-stratosphere. In doing so, he discovered the existence of the jet stream.

His career was assisted by a friendship with American humorist Will Rogers, whom Post met in 1925 while flying the writer to a rodeo. Rogers subsequently gave the aviator considerable free publicity, and in return Post provided him with flights across North America. It was on one of these excursions that an accident ended both of their lives; in August 1935, as Post and Rogers took off from Point Barrow, Alaska, the engine of their plane stalled – it careened back to earth, killing both men. Rogers, whose life was marked by his success as an actor,

A transatlantic flight with blatant political overtones was that of the Justice for Hungary *(see below and opposite in Harbour Grace). Its financiers used the flight to draw attention to Hungary's territorial losses following the First World War.*

author, pundit, and philosopher, was memorialised by the *New York Times* as "the most widely-known citizen of the US ... and the best beloved."

Post was motivated by several factors, including money, prestige, and a competitive drive, to break speed and endurance records. Patriotic fervour inspired many other attempts at flying across the Atlantic, but none would match the absurdity of a Hungarian effort in 1931 that almost ended in a shoot-out.

The goal of flying from Harbour Grace to Budapest was designed to bring attention to the dismantlement of Hungary through the Treaty of Trianon after the First World War. Many Hungarians remained bitter about losing two-thirds of their country to the newly established nations of Czechoslovakia, Romania, and Yugoslavia.

Among them were two Hungarian reserve pilots, Sándor Wilczek and György Endres, who would bring attention to this issue by flying non-stop from Newfoundland to Hungary. Both men had recently emigrated to North America, but like many Hungarian expatriates they identified closely with their native country. In fact, when Wilczek immigrated after the war, he changed his surname to Magyar, which literally means a native of Hungary. Endres, who served with the Austro-Hungarian air force during the war, had been Magyar's flight instructor.

Magyar moved to Windsor, Ontario, where he boarded with a clergyman, William Molnar, who encouraged him to follow his dream of flying to his homeland. He claimed to have been convinced when Molnar opened the Bible at random and came upon the line, "These things ye shall do unto the Lord ..."

A Michigan meat-packing businessman, Emil Szalay, raised US $20,000 by mortgaging his business; he turned the proceeds over to Endres, who purchased a Lockheed Sirius aircraft, identical to one owned by Charles and Anne Lindbergh. Szalay said the commitment fulfilled a promise made to his father many years earlier that he would "do something for Hungary".

Aside from bringing attention to their cause, Endres and Magyar were also hoping to win the prize money offered by one of Hungary's most influential European supporters, Harold Harmsworth, who was given the title Viscount Rothermere in 1919. In 1917, Prime Minister Lloyd George had appointed the British newspaper tycoon as President of the Air Council, which was the precursor to the Royal Air Force.

Harmsworth and his brother Alfred owned the *Daily Mail* and several other influential newspapers; by 1926 Rothermere had become one of the richest men in Great Britain. During the 1930s he would become a prominent supporter of appeasement with Adolf Hitler.

The Harmsworths were also well known in Newfoundland where they had operated a pulp and paper mill in Grand Falls since 1909; their Anglo-American Development Company provided a cheap supply of newsprint for their newspapers.

From the early days of aviation the Harmsworths had also been synonymous with aircraft, offering cash prizes for several pioneering feats. Among the most notable was a £10,000 *Daily Mail* award for flying non-stop across the Atlantic, which was won by Alcock and Brown in 1919.

After the war, Rothermere became a supporter of the Hungarian cause, and in 1930 he offered US $10,000 to the first Hungarian to fly non-stop from North America to Budapest, Hungary's capital. Rothermere took a particular interest in the bid by Endres and Magyar, even choosing a name for their plane, *Justice for Hungary*.

The aircraft, with Endres and Magyar in the cockpit, left Roosevelt Field on July 13 and arrived in Harbour Grace later that evening. They were greeted by a small group of Hungarians who had travelled to Newfoundland to support their compatriots. Several prominent members of the St John's political and business elite joined them in Harbour Grace.

Two days later the *Justice for Hungary* took off for Europe. Although the transatlantic leg of the flight was uneventful, the plane had used more fuel than anticipated.

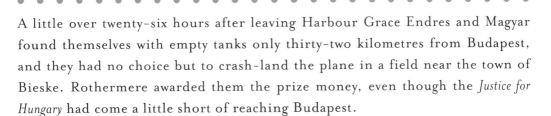

Family members of transoceanic flyers endured the stress of waiting for the safe arrival of their loved ones. Elizabeth Endres is pictured in her home on July 15, 1931, anxiously awaiting news about her son, György Endres, who, with Sándor Wilczek, was flying over the Atlantic, en route to Budapest.

A little over twenty-six hours after leaving Harbour Grace Endres and Magyar found themselves with empty tanks only thirty-two kilometres from Budapest, and they had no choice but to crash-land the plane in a field near the town of Bieske. Rothermere awarded them the prize money, even though the *Justice for Hungary* had come a little short of reaching Budapest.

Hungarians initially rejoiced at the achievement. The nation's armed forces awarded promotions to both Endres and Magyar, and large crowds greeted the pilots at public events. But public feuding soon replaced the initial goodwill, as questions arose about Magyar's past. It was suggested that their hero had changed his name and fled Hungary in order to avoid repercussions arising from "misconduct". The nature of this claim is unclear, but with his honour besmirched

Magyar responded by challenging six members of Budapest's sporting society to a duel. Whether he intended to fight them in succession or as a group is not known, but a settlement was reached without resorting to violence.

Trouble arose once again, however, when Szalay sold the *Justice for Hungary*. After reimbursing himself for expenses associated with the flight, he proposed splitting the surplus between the two flyers. By now, however, Endres was no longer on speaking terms with Magyar and told Szalay that he alone was entitled to the money. This enraged Magyar, who challenged Endres to yet another duel. Endres accepted. According to the two men, fighting a duel was the only acceptable way for Hungarian military officers to settle such disputes.

At this point the Hungarian Aviation Society intervened and pleaded with the men to call off the duel. The aviators eventually conceded and Magyar returned to the United States. But Endres would not enjoy his success for long; he was killed in May 1932 while landing an aircraft in Rome. He had travelled there to attend an aviators' convention, hosted by the Italian president, Benito Mussolini.

By 1932 the Depression had reached its lowest point, as North America and Europe buckled under the weight of mass unemployment and economic devastation. Perhaps in response to these economic difficulties the public yearned for entertainment in all its forms, including stunt flying and air races. But the cash prizes that fuelled pioneer flight throughout the 1920s had become increasingly scarce due to difficulties obtaining sponsors from cash-starved businesses. In addition, there were few "firsts" left to be achieved in conventional aviation.

So there was considerable interest within the aviation fraternity when a Norwegian newspaper offered US $10,000 for the first non-stop flight to Oslo from North America. In August 1932 a race began between two teams of flyers.

One team consisted of Carl Petersen and Thor Solberg, both of whom had been born in Norway and had moved to the United States. Petersen previously travelled twice to the Antarctic with Richard Byrd and played a significant role in advancing the science of radio communications. In 1932 Petersen, who owned a Bellanca aircraft, convinced the Enna Jettick shoe company to sponsor his flight, and in recognition of this support he named his plane *Enna Jettick*.

Their competition was a Wisconsin pilot, Clyde Lee, and his Norwegian-born navigator, John Bochkon. Lee was known as "Daredevil Lee" because he performed stunts such as walking along the wing of an aircraft while it was in flight. Lee was unable to obtain financial support for the transatlantic journey in Wisconsin. But a Vermont cement manufacturer agreed to pay the expenses, provided the Stinson monoplane was christened *Green Mountain Boy*. This name was chosen to honour a group of soldiers from Vermont who had fought in the American Revolutionary War.

On August 23 the transatlantic race began, with the *Enna Jettick* starting from Floyd Bennett Field, New York, and the *Green Mountain Boy* from Barre, Vermont. A further dramatic touch was added when both crews disclosed that they were planning a stop at Harbour Grace before heading to Norway.

But the highly anticipated race ended only a few hours after it began. Navigation became difficult as the hazards of rain, fog, and snow enveloped both aircraft as they flew over southern Newfoundland. Lee managed to land the *Green Mountain Boy* on a beach in the coastal community of Burgeo.

The crew of the *Enna Jettick* were not so lucky. As the sky darkened towards evening, Petersen and Solberg looked for a safe open space to land their plane. They spotted lights over Placentia Bay on southeast coast of Newfoundland, but while descending, Solberg suddenly noticed a hillside looming into view. But too late he banked sharply to avoid disaster, and in doing so one of the plane's wings struck the water. The *Enna Jettick* finished its journey tail-up in the fishing village of Darby's Harbour. Petersen and Solberg survived the accident unscathed.

The next day, August 24, the *Green Mountain Boy* left Burgeo and landed at Harbour Grace. A day later, Lee and Bochkon set out for Norway. Although weather forecasts provided to the pilots were favourable, in reality a massive fog bank had enveloped much of northern Europe. The fog was so dense that all flights in Great Britain had been cancelled. In Wales, there were reports of people hearing an aircraft engine, and it was later speculated that it belonged to the *Green Mountain Boy* since all flights had been grounded due to the fog. There was no confirmation, however, and neither the plane nor Lee and Bochkon were seen again.

But Solberg would get a second chance to reach Norway by air. In 1935 he and Paul Oscanyan successfully flew a Loening amphibious aircraft, named *Leif Eiriksson*, on a northern route to Bergen. The 8,500-kilometre journey from New York included stops in the Labrador community of Cartwright, as well as Greenland, Iceland, and the Faroe Islands.

In the mid-1930s several other European nations became the focus of transatlantic aviation. On July 15, 1933, Lithuanian American pilots Stephan Darius and Stanley Girenas took off from Floyd Bennett Field in a plane name *Lituanica*, bound for Kaunas, Lithuania. For several hours, the flight proceeded without incident, as the *Lituanica* passed over Newfoundland, but bad weather forced them north of their planned flight path over the Atlantic. Although the pilots managed to get back on course over Germany, they were killed when their plane crashed near the town of Pszczelnik, Poland – then known as Soldin, Germany. Since no mechanical failures were found and the plane still had fuel on board, investigators theorised that the men had fallen asleep.

The race to fly non-stop to Poland had begun inauspiciously a year earlier, in 1932, when Stanislaus Hausner was forced to ditch his plane in the ocean and wait several days inside the wreck before being rescued. In 1934, it seemed that Polish honour would be restored by two native sons – until US authorities decided to probe the business activities of the erstwhile heroes.

Benjamin and Joseph Adamowicz were teenagers when their widowed mother moved with them to Brooklyn, New York, from Poland in 1911. The boys, who found work in a bottling plant, later opened their own soda water bottling business on Long Island.

Like many people who became enamoured with aviation, the Adamowicz brothers were inspired by the New York-Paris race in 1927, which was won by Charles Lindbergh. They were among thousands of people who visited airfields across the United States and paid money to experience the thrill of flying. After being a passenger on one of these short flights, Benjamin reportedly told Joseph, "I can do that." Both men then earned their pilot's licence.

While many people dreamed of flying across the Atlantic, the Adamowicz brothers were among the few to actively pursue this quest. In 1933, they hired Holger Hoiriis, who had flown to Denmark from Newfoundland in the *Liberty* two years earlier. Hoiriis gave them further instruction, including valuable advice on flying the treacherous skies of the North Atlantic.

The Adamowicz brothers purchased the *Liberty* from Hoiriis and re-named it *White Eagle* – a white eagle being on Poland's official coat of arms. On August 7, 1933, they and pilot Emile Bergen flew to Harbour Grace. The following day the three men boarded the *White Eagle* and prepared for takeoff. As the plane

"It's the money I need. A good engine, and it would be a cinch." Clyde Lee, on flying across the Atlantic.

gained speed, however, it suddenly veered off the runway and crashed into the brush. The three men were not seriously injured, but the plane was badly damaged and they were forced to return to New York.

Despite this failure, the brothers were determined to try again the following year. After the plane had been repaired, Hoiriis taught them how to fly using instruments

• •

Clyde Lee (top) was a daredevil who thrilled crowds at air shows with his "wingwalker" stunt. His decision to fly from Harbour Grace (above right) to Norway would prove to be his undoing, however, as both he and co-pilot John Bochkon disappeared over the north Atlantic. Left: Bochkon and Lee.

• •

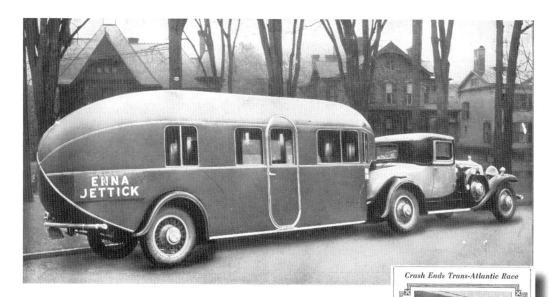

Right: An image from the Toronto Telegram of the men competing to reach Oslo, Norway, (left to right) John Bochkon and Clyde Lee (insert), Thor Solberg, and Carl Petersen. Below: The Enna Jettick ended its journey at Darby's Harbour, Newfoundland. The flight was sponsored by the Enna Jettick shoe company, which also promoted its wares using a trailer (above) designed by aircraft engineer Glenn Curtiss — builder of the Navy Curtiss flying boats that reached the Azores in 1919.

Crash Ends Trans-Atlantic Race

A RACE BETWEEN TWO MONOPLANES to cross the Atlantic came to an end with the wreck of one ship at Placentia Bay, Newfoundland. The second plane landed far west of Harbour Grace, where both had planned to refuel, but missed their objective when storms and fog obscured landing beacons. Pictures show John Bochkon and Clyde A. Lee, crew of the "Green Mountain Boy," which landed safely and which is continuing its flight from Barre, Vermont, to Oslo, Norway. INSET, Thor Solberg and Carl Petersen, crew of the plane which crashed.

alone — a lifesaving skill when travelling through fog and darkness. On June 28, 1934, Hoiriis accompanied Benjamin and Joseph to Harbour Grace. The plane, which had been renamed *City of Warsaw*, took off without incident the next day with only the brothers on board. Hoiriis returned to New York.

Unlike many of their predecessors, the brothers experienced only minor difficulties crossing the Grand Banks of Newfoundland. Their luck ran out, however, as the *City of Warsaw* neared France, when a severe storm drove them off course. After flying blindly through fog for three hours, they finally found land. The plane was down to its last few minutes of fuel when the pilots sighted what they thought was Ireland. They were wrong. The plane had actually landed in a pasture at the village of St André de Messel, eighty kilometres from Caen in northern France.

The brothers flew to Paris the next day and hoped to reach Warsaw after a few hours of flight. News of their imminent arrival swept through Poland, and some 15,000 people waited anxiously for the Adamowiczs' arrival at Warsaw's military airport. Difficulties continued to plague the aviators, however, as the plane ran out of fuel over Germany, forcing them to land in a potato field near the Polish border.

Finally, on July 2 the plane landed in Warsaw, although not before it made another unplanned stop in the Polish city of Torun. A squadron of bombers accompanied the *City of Warsaw* as it approached the capital; the US ambassador greeted them at the airport, after which the brothers were taken on a procession to City Hall.

The Adamowicz brothers enjoyed two months basking as celebrities in the nation of their birth. They even profited from their exploits by selling the *City of Warsaw* to a museum. On September 23, the brothers boarded a passenger ship at Gdynia, and bade farewell to thousands of cheering spectators. "We're going back to the soda water business in Brooklyn," Joseph said before they left Poland. "But we won't neglect flying, and we hope to fly back to Warsaw without stopping en-route."

But their triumphant departure masked trouble at home. A day before the Adamowicz brothers left Poland, New York police had swooped into their bottling plant, which was being run during their absence by another brother, Bronislaw. It seems that soda water was not the only beverage being bottled on the premises; the authorities announced that they had raided the largest illegal still ever uncovered on Long Island.

The Adamowicz brothers damaged the White Eagle *on take off from Harbour Grace in 1933. Their Bellanca aircraft had previously flown to Denmark in 1931 under the name* Liberty.

The three brothers protested their innocence in the face of overwhelming evidence. They claimed that a man named Schwartz had rented part of their business; however, investigators could find no record of this person. A jury was unable to reach a verdict in the first trial, but in April 1935 all three were convicted. They were sentenced to fifteen months in jail.

The motivations of those such as the Adamowicz brothers who attempted to fly across the Atlantic during the early years of flight fell loosely into the following categories: money, patriotism, personal glory, and thirst for adventure.

In 1936, Scottish flying hero James Mollison would add another reason – revenge. Mollison had burst into prominence in 1931 by setting a record of almost nine days for flying to England from Australia. Rather fittingly, he

landed near Hastings, where William the Conquerer first set foot in 1066 — the last successful military invasion of England.

But it was Mollison's love life that captured the public's imagination. The consummate ladies' man had been engaged to a young aristocrat until he met Amy Johnson, a former secretary who shared his love for flying. Johnson had completed pilot training in the late 1920s, and soon began setting records of her own. In 1930, she became the first woman to fly solo from Great Britain to Australia, and in 1932 she broke the speed record for flying to South Africa from Britain.

She and Mollison were soon married. To celebrate their nuptials, Mollison announced that he would become the first person to achieve a solo flight westward

Top: After repairing their plane, which was re-christened the City of Warsaw, *the Adamowicz brothers returned to Harbour Grace in 1934. Above right: Benjamin and Joseph Adamowicz (fourth and fifth from left) reached Europe on their second try, but had to stop in France after running low on fuel.*

across the Atlantic, from Ireland to New York City. The newlywed aptly named his aircraft *Heart's Content*. Mollison came close to succeeding in his quest, but his plane ran out of fuel before reaching New York. He had flown from Ireland to Pennfield Ridge, New Brunswick, a community near Saint John, in thirty hours.

In 1933 the record-setting couple embarked upon their most ambitious project, flying the Atlantic together, from Wales to New York. The duo almost made it, but unfortunately their aircraft, named *Seafarer*, ran out of fuel at Bridgeport, Connecticut, only minutes from New York City. Both pilots suffered minor injuries as the plane ploughed into the ground and overturned.

But the public image of a happy couple, participating in wild adventures, turned out to be a façade. Their marriage was foundering, as Mollison enjoyed the company of women other than his wife. The first public hint of discord came in May 1936 when Johnson flew solo on a return flight between England and Cape Town. In doing so she demolished the previous record set by her husband, making the journey in just four days and sixteen hours. Mollison was not among the large crowd that greeted Johnson upon her return.

After surviving an air crash in October that year Johnson publicly disclosed that she and her husband had separated. This unwelcome publicity infuriated Mollison. But the scorned husband responded in a unique fashion: he would attempt to set a new speed record for flying across the Atlantic, and then immediately smash the mark set months earlier by his estranged wife for a return flight between England and Cape Town.

On October 28, just days after Johnson's revelation about their marital difficulties, Mollison flew from New York and arrived in Harbour Grace hours later. He was flying a newly acquired Bellanca 28-70 monoplane which he named *Dorothy* in honour of Dorothy Ward, an actress with whom he was having a relationship. The flamboyant aviator climbed from the cockpit in Harbour Grace wearing a stylish dinner jacket, but he was in no mood to discuss his flight from New York. "I am cold and tired," was all he told reporters before seeking refuge in his hotel room.

Mollison took off the next day. He arrived safely at Croydon airport thirteen hours and seventeen minutes later, thereby setting a new speed record for crossing the Atlantic. In doing so, he had also become the first person to fly across the ocean four times. True to form, Mollison displayed his penchant for high living after stepping from his plane. "I am so damned tired," he said, while caressing a

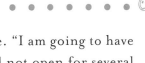

James Mollison and the Dorothy, *a Bellanca Flash, in Harbour Grace prior to setting a speed record for flying across the Atlantic Ocean.*

lucky rabbit's foot, given to him by a girl in Harbour Grace. "I am going to have a large scotch and soda." As drinking establishments would not open for several hours, Mollison had to settle for ginger beer.

He may have crossed the Atlantic in record time, but the grudge flight to South Africa and back would have to wait. First, Mollison decided to visit Ward at her home in Edinburgh. Then, the Bellanca Aircraft Corporation seized his plane, pending payment of the balance outstanding on purchase of the machine. Finally, a month after arriving in London, Mollison had settled with Bellanca and was ready to challenge his wife's record. Unlike Johnson, who flew solo, he hired a co-pilot, Edouard Corniglion-Molinier. He and Mollison had previously flown together while conducting aerial surveys for archeologists in northern Africa. The French flying ace led a remarkable military career, winning the Croix de Guerre in both world wars.

The two men took off from Croydon Airport on November 29. Despite some delays, they remained on a record-setting pace — until losing their way in South Africa. They were listed as missing for several days, but were eventually found just 160 kilometres from Cape Town. Johnson's record had withstood the challenge.

With the advent of the Second World War both Mollison and Johnson joined the British Air Transport Authority, ferrying aircraft from factories to air bases.

While flying a mission in January 1941, Johnson was forced to ditch into the Thames estuary after overshooting her destination and running out of fuel. She drowned before a rescue craft could reach her.

Mollison survived the war, but alcoholism exacted its toll on his health. He died in 1959 at the age of fifty-four. Corniglion-Molinier would continue to lead a successful, varied career; he became a film producer after the war, and then entered politics, where he served in several cabinet posts.

By the mid-1930s, advances in aviation technology and aircraft safety had greatly reduced the element of danger for pilots and passengers. Airlines throughout North America and Europe were competing for airmail contracts and several companies offered passenger flights between major cities to the few who could afford tickets.

However, flying across the world's oceans remained exceptionally dangerous, as one of America's leading entertainers would find out in 1936. Nightclub singer Harry Richman had soared to fame during the 1920s, sharing the stage with such stars as Mae West. The "King of Broadway" enjoyed a string of popular records, as well as a torrid relationship with the original "It Girl", Clara Bow.

Richman's success gave him the means to engage in the expensive hobby of aviation. He became friends with American First World War flying ace, Eddie Rickenbacker, who had since become a senior executive with Eastern Air Lines. The two men had more than aviation in common; during the First World War both had changed the spelling of their Germanic surnames – from Reichman and Reichenbacher.

Richman was determined to achieve one of the few unclaimed transatlantic records: the first round-trip flight by plane between the US and Europe. On September 2, 1936, he and Eastern Air Lines pilot Henry T (Dick) Merrill took off from Floyd Bennett Field in Brooklyn, New York, bound for London. Richman stated that he would have tea in the British capital, and then dine on Broadway after returning to New York the following evening.

For the voyage, Richman and Merrill flew a Vultee VI-A, a single-engine aircraft used by American Air Lines for its US passenger routes in the early 1930s. Richman drew attention to rising political tensions in Europe by naming his plane *Lady Peace*. He also underlined the danger of the flight by stowing a load of 41,000 ping-pong balls into cavities within the wings of the plane, to make the craft more buoyant in case he and Merrill were forced to ditch it at sea.

Although the flight to Europe was largely uneventful, Merrill lost his way as

Amy Johnson exacted revenge against her cheating husband,
James Mollison, by beating his record for a return flight between
England and South Africa.

The Dorothy flying over Brooklyn, New York, prior to Mollison's 1936 flight.

the *Lady Peace* neared land. The plane had run low on fuel by the time the men finally sighted the British Isles, following an eighteen-hour journey. After looking for suitable terrain in Wales, Merrill landed the plane safely in a field at the village of Llwyncelyn. Richman told the *New York Times*:

We picked a field where there were three cows. Those cows sure were ladylike and knew good manners. They trotted off nicely as we came down and nobody minded.

A day later the *Lady Peace* arrived at Croydon Airport in London. The ping-pong balls drew the attention of British customs authorities, who debated whether to charge duty on the merchandise since the items were categorised as sporting goods. They finally agreed to accept the flyers' argument that the ping-pong balls were being carried as equipment and Richman was not compelled to pay import duties.

Any notions the men had of refuelling the plane and immediately returning to New York had been dismissed by the time they reached London. The flyers were exhausted. Besides, Richman quickly became the toast of London high society, so the flamboyant showman decided to delay his return flight by a few days.

Inclement weather forced Richman and Merrill to extend their stay even longer. But on September 14, after finally receiving reports of clear skies over the entire North Atlantic, the *Lady Peace* departed Southport, England, on a projected non-stop return trip to New York. But the weather predictions turned out to be highly inaccurate, and during the flight stormy weather and dense fog drove the aircraft off course. With their fuel supply running low, Merrill was forced to make an emergency landing in Newfoundland. After fruitlessly searching for Harbour Grace airfield, he opted to land near Musgrave Harbour, a community on the northeast coast of Newfoundland.

The plane rolled along the grass before sinking into a peat bog, however, although its nose tipped forward into the ground, the plane was largely undamaged. Fishermen mending their nets on shore hurried on foot over rough terrain to reach the aircraft. They raised the stricken machine from the marsh by sliding timbers under its wheels. Richman reportedly remarked as he drank tea before an open fire:

That Newfoundland bog is sure soft stuff. It sunk in like a feather bed, it seemed to me, and felt just about as good.

Upon learning of Richman's woes, Rickenbacker organised a rescue party. Two Eastern Air Lines planes left New York for Musgrave Harbour with mechanics and spare parts. But the Americans were unfamiliar with Newfoundland place names, and mistakenly landed at Musgravetown, about 120 kilometres south of Musgrave Harbour.

When Rickenbacker and his team finally arrived on the beach at Musgrave Harbour, they quickly repaired the *Lady Peace*. The machine was then dragged out of the mire onto a specially built wooden runway. Merrill and Richman flew to Harbour Grace, and then finished their journey to New York. They arrived at Floyd Bennett Field on September 21, and in spite of the extensive delays and numerous mishaps the flyers had achieved the first round-trip crossing of the Atlantic Ocean by plane.

But Richman's record would soon be tested, this time by his pilot, Merrill, who gained valuable experience flying both directions across the Atlantic. The coronation of King George VI in May 1937 offered a unique opportunity for two Wall Street businessmen, Ben Smith and Jack Bergen, who would use the event to attempt the first commercial round-trip flight by aircraft.

The men believed they could earn headlines while turning a considerable profit by flying a plane non-stop to London, collecting photographs and film footage of the coronation, and then immediately flying the images back to New York where they had an eager buyer in William Randolph Hearst and his news-paper empire.

Smith and Bergen purchased a Lockheed Electra, which they named *Daily Express* in honour of Smith's friend Lord Beaverbrook who owned a newspaper of the same name. The promoters also convinced Eastern Air Lines to release Merrill and another pilot, John Lambie, for the journey.

The plan seemed to be working flawlessly until government officials took note of the journey. Monroe Johnson, Assistant Secretary of Commerce, argued that this and other transatlantic flights were mere stunts and warned that a ban was being contemplated by the Bureau of Air Commerce, the nation's aviation

regulator, in order to curtail what he termed "freak flights".

But tragedy intervened. On May 6, the course of aviation history changed when the *Hindenburg* airship erupted into flames over New Jersey, just days before the coronation. While the accident ended the era of the airship, it diverted Monroe from the *Daily Express* controversy; he immediately took charge of an official inquiry into the *Hindenburg* disaster

● ●

Opposite: A misunderstanding of local nomenclature complicated the rescue of Broadway singer Harry Richman's plane from a bog at Musgrave Harbour, Newfoundland. Opposite left: A team, led by US First World War flying-ace, Eddie Rickenbacker (centre), mistakenly landed at Musgravetown, 125 kilometres away. Eventually, the Lady Peace *— with Richman (right) and pilot Dick Merrill (left) — was extricated and flown to Harbour Grace. Rickenbacker worked for Eastern Airlines, and flew one of the company's DC-2 aircraft, known collectively as The Great Silver Fleet. Opposite bottom left: Sheet music featuring Harry Richman.*

● ●

and did not ban the flight by Merrill and Lambie.

Coincidentally, the disaster gave the flight's promoters new business prospects, as they collected dramatic photographs and film footage of the *Hindenburg* explosion to sell to English news outlets. With the valuable merchandise safely stowed away, Merrill and Lambie took off from Floyd Bennett Field on May 10 and arrived at Croydon Airfield after a largely uneventful flight.

But Smith and Bergen soon had some of their hopes dashed by British censors. While photographs of the *Hindenburg* explosion were free to be distributed, newsreel footage was not. "London has banned the films because it doesn't want a shadow cast over the coronation ceremonies," Smith complained.

After the coronation, Merrill and Lambie received another unwelcome surprise as they prepared to take photographs and film footage back to New York. Again, the British government intervened and refused to allow newsreels out of the country.

The *Daily Express* left England on May 14 and arrived in New York, thereby achieving the first commercial round trip by an aircraft and the fastest two-way crossing of the Atlantic. They were greeted by thousands of people, and as they disembarked from their automobile at the Waldorf Hotel a young woman named Zymade Spurrell rushed forward and kissed Merrill on his cheek — much to his embarrassment.

Among those who celebrated this flight was Eddie Rickenbacker of Eastern Air Lines, who saw the achievement as a herald of the future. He told the *New York Times*:

I believe that in three years or less there will be regular commercial flights between Europe and the United States by airplane. The flight by Merrill and Lambie has proved that it is possible to have a speedy and dependable service between the continents.

The Lady Peace *and Eddie Rickenbacker's DC-2 at Harbour Grace.*

CHAPTER 8
INCREDIBLE RESCUES

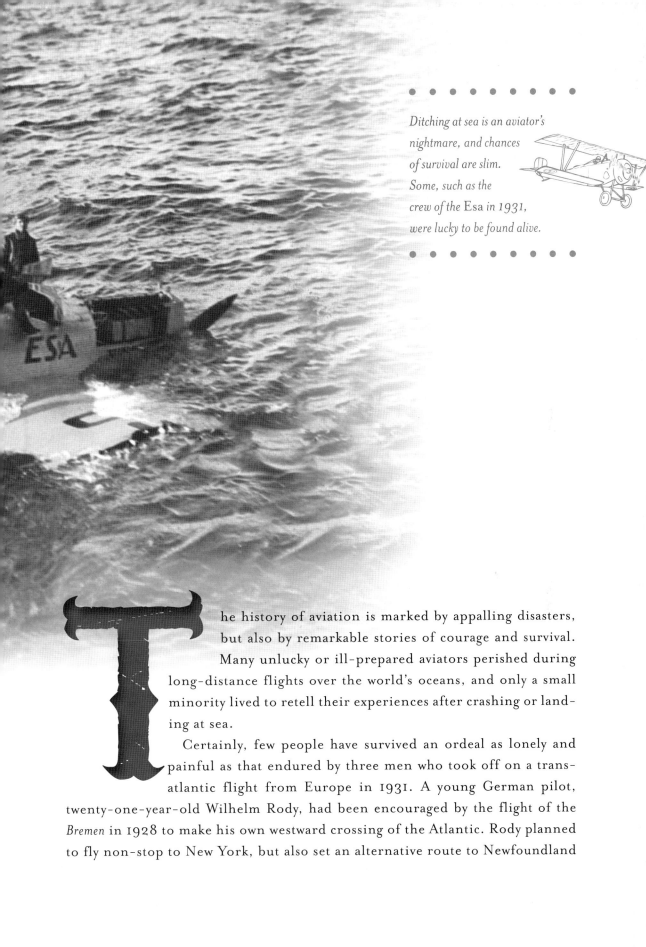

The history of aviation is marked by appalling disasters, but also by remarkable stories of courage and survival. Many unlucky or ill-prepared aviators perished during long-distance flights over the world's oceans, and only a small minority lived to retell their experiences after crashing or landing at sea.

Certainly, few people have survived an ordeal as lonely and painful as that endured by three men who took off on a transatlantic flight from Europe in 1931. A young German pilot, twenty-one-year-old Wilhelm Rody, had been encouraged by the flight of the *Bremen* in 1928 to make his own westward crossing of the Atlantic. Rody planned to fly non-stop to New York, but also set an alternative route to Newfoundland

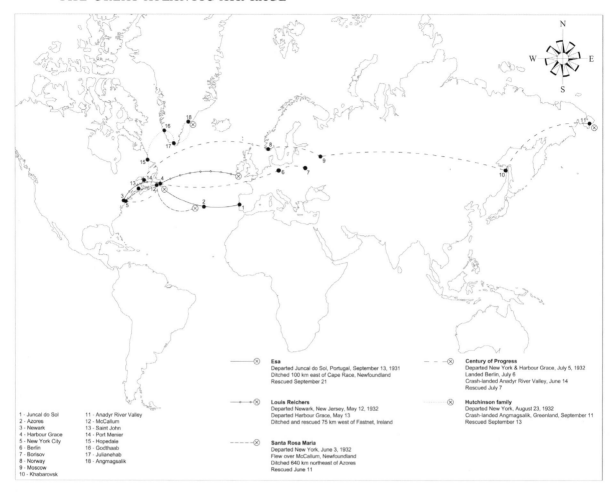

Esa
Departed Juncal do Sol, Portugal, September 13, 1931
Ditched 100 km east of Cape Race, Newfoundland
Rescued September 21

Louis Reichers
Departed Newark, New Jersey, May 12, 1932
Departed Harbour Grace, May 13
Ditched and rescued 75 km west of Fastnet, Ireland

Santa Rosa Maria
Departed New York, June 3, 1932
Flew over McCallum, Newfoundland
Ditched 640 km northeast of Azores
Rescued June 11

Century of Progress
Departed New York & Harbour Grace, July 5, 1932
Landed Berlin, July 6
Crash-landed Anadyr River Valley, June 14
Rescued July 7

Hutchinson family
Departed New York, August 23, 1932
Crash-landed Angmagsalik, Greenland, September 11
Rescued September 13

1 - Juncal do Sol
2 - Azores
3 - Newark
4 - Harbour Grace
5 - New York City
6 - Berlin
7 - Borisov
8 - Norway
9 - Moscow
10 - Khabarovsk
11 - Anadyr River Valley
12 - McCallum
13 - Saint John
14 - Port Menier
15 - Hopedale
16 - Godthaab
17 - Julianehab
18 - Angmagsalik

if the weather deteriorated. After reaching New York, he intended to fly back to Europe and thereby achieve the first round trip of the Atlantic by a heavier-than-air aircraft.

He used inheritance money to purchase a German-made Junkers W-33 aircraft, and hired a former First World War flyer, Christian Johanssen, to be his co-pilot. A Portuguese passenger, Fernando da Costa Viega, also accompanied them.

The plane was named *Esa*, after Rody's fiancée, and following a christening ceremony on September 13, 1931, at Juncal do Sol in Portugal, the *Esa* took off with Rody and his companions. The men calculated that the *Esa* was carrying enough fuel to last forty-eight hours; the flyers also brought provisions: 12 bananas, 24 apples, sandwiches, and 3 loaves of bread. "Plenty," Rody said, prior to the flight, "to last us until we get there."

If the plane was forced to land on the ocean, Rody expected it could float for eight hours. Rather than carry a radio, the flyers opted to stow an additional drum of gasoline into the fuselage — a decision they would later regret.

On the day it took off, the *Esa* was seen flying over the Azores and again on September 14 by a passenger liner, the *Pennland*, 130 kilometres east of Cape Race, Newfoundland. This was the last sighting of the aircraft. Search planes were soon sent to scour the ocean, but their efforts were in vain. As the days passed, hope gave way to acceptance that the men were dead. So the world reacted with shock when, on September 21, all three were plucked alive from the plane's wreckage by the crew of a passing freighter. They were found thirteen kilometres off the coast of Newfoundland.

Fortunately, Rody had vastly underestimated how long the aircraft could float. Rather than eight hours, they had been drifting helplessly in the ocean for more than six days on what remained of the plane's disintegrating fuselage. The men were in remarkably good physical condition, although Viega was suffering from exposure and a leg injury.

• •

After spending six days marooned near the coast of Newfoundland with their disintegrating aircraft, a Soviet freighter rescued the three adventurers who flew the Esa.

• •

In relating their ordeal, Rody said the flight had gone well until they passed the Azores. At that point strong headwinds started buffeting the plane, so he and Johanssen decided to fly to Newfoundland rather than continue on to New York.

But powerful winds continued to challenge the *Esa*. A cold front then moved in, and soon the pilots were battling a powerful storm. Rody told the *New York Times*:

> Whirlwinds rocked us back and forth. They tossed us and battered at us so that we could not keep a straight course. Again and again we were hammered about in a circle.

Adding to their troubles, one of the six cylinders of the single-engine plane ceased working. The engine sputtered as the *Esa* struggled through the night. Worse yet, the engine would only function at full throttle, which meant that the plane was consuming fuel at an alarming rate.

In the morning the men were overjoyed to see the *Pennland*. Judging from the ship's course, Rody knew that the *Esa* was nearing land. The plane circled overhead, delighting passengers who had no idea that the *Esa* had suffered mechanical damage. Despite the plane's engine problems, Rody said he and the other two men never considered ditching the *Esa* alongside the ship.

> We had had our chance of immediate safety, with that liner so close, but not one of us thought of our lives. We wanted to reach America in our plane and to land there.

So the *Esa* kept going — charging directly into the wind. Two hours later the fuel supply, which had lasted thirty-six rather than forty-eight hours, was gone. The engine coughed to a halt, and without power the plane drifted towards the ocean waves.

Our feeling was indescribable. Suspense tightened and twisted our nerves. We looked at each other. We looked at that ocean.

As the plane dropped into the crest of a wave Rody, Johanssen, and Viega opened the cabin door and scrambled onto the fuselage. They watched as the wings filled with water, and parts of the plane were ripped away by tumultuous ocean swells. The men lay on their stomachs, grasping desperately to remain with the stricken craft as the sea became rougher. Suddenly, a large wave demolished the cabin door, washing away all of their food and fresh water.

As night came, the men felt the cold eating away at them through their soaked clothing. They retreated to the cabin, only to find it half full of water. Rody said later:

Never shall we forget this night, or the nights that followed before our rescue. The first night we spent standing in rising water in the little cabin.

For the next six days, the men had only seven ounces of chocolate for food, and drank oily water from the engine's cooling system. As the days passed, the men grew weaker and Viega, whose leg had been injured as the plane was being tossed about in the air, became feverish. All of them found their skin peeling and their legs swelling from standing in water day after day. The plane was also disintegrating around them, and each day it sank a little lower beneath the water.

No ship passed them for over five days. Then, on September 20 they saw a freighter. Rody recalled:

We waved our flag 'til all strength had left us, but that ship never saw us. It was unbelievable.

Despair set in, but the next day they spied another vessel. The men signalled

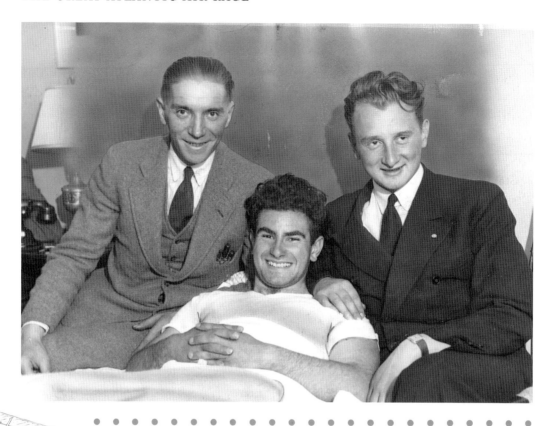

Despite their ordeal on the Esa, *the crewmen were largely unharmed. From left: Christian Johanssen, Fernando da Costa Viega, and Wilhelm Rody.*

again and watched apprehensively. It turned towards them; they'd been seen. "We were saved," Rody said.

The ship, which was carrying locomotives to the Soviet Union, transferred the airmen to a passenger liner heading to New York. Upon their arrival, Viega spent several days in hospital, where he made a complete recovery. Although Rody pledged to make another transatlantic attempt, there is no record of him doing so.

Unlike Rody and his companions, few of the aviators who failed in their attempts to cross the North Atlantic lived to recount their experiences. By 1932 twenty had died, with no bodies recovered and little wreckage found. Only the crew of the *Esa*, and Hawker and Mackenzie-Grieve in 1919, had survived a plunge into the icy waters between Newfoundland and Ireland – until 1932 when

American air racer Louis Reichers set out from Harbour Grace.

Like many professional pilots of his era, Reichers financed his passion for flight by flying passenger planes and contracting his services to wealthy businessmen. One of his clients was Bernarr Macfadden, a controversial but successful health food and exercise guru. Macfadden, who had changed his name from Bernard MacFadden, also published several sensational magazines, including *True Detective* and *True Story*.

Starting in 1930 Reichers began challenging speed and endurance records. After flying with Macfadden on a tour of Europe in 1931, Reichers was ready to make an attempt at breaking Lindbergh's record for flying from New York to Paris. Macfadden loaned Reichers one of his aircraft, a Lockheed Altair. Reichers changed its name from *Gold Eagle* to *Liberty* and had an image of the Statue of Liberty painted onto the plane's fuselage.

Reichers left Newark, New Jersey, in the *Liberty* at 11:00 p.m. on May 12, and arrived in Harbour Grace in a record time of six hours and nineteen minutes. He refuelled the aircraft, repaired some minor damage to the plane's stabiliser, and, within a few hours, set out for Europe. Reichers planned to land at Baldonnel Airfield in Dublin before finishing his journey at Le Bourget Airport in Paris.

The first hour passed without incident, but, as he crossed the Grand Banks of Newfoundland, a thick layer of cloud enveloped the *Liberty*. After flying almost blind for more than ten hours, Reichers lost hope of reaching Ireland. As night approached, and with little fuel remaining, he searched the ocean for the lights of a ship. Finally, he spotted a passenger liner, the *President Roosevelt*, and signalled the crew that he was about to ditch the plane and needed to be rescued. Reichers slowed the plane and landed with a jolt in the ocean. He later wrote:

It was very dark and visibility so poor that I had to hang my head out to see when landing. As I needed both hands to land, I could not protect my face, and the shock threw me forward, hitting the cowl; but outside of bending my nose out of shape — that required two stitches to straighten — there was no other damage.

After air racer Louis Reichers (above and opposite) was forced to ditch his aircraft in the Atlantic
Ocean, he was rescued by a passenger ship, the President Roosevelt (opposite
top). Three years earlier, in 1928, the liner had carried Amelia Earhart back to the
US after she became the first woman to fly across the Atlantic.

Reichers had come tantalizingly close to success; he was rescued only seventy-five kilometres west of the Irish coast.

Reichers said Macfadden radioed him aboard the ship and reported that his sponsor was not concerned about losing the plane. After returning to the United States Reichers focused on being a test pilot, a risky occupation he had embarked upon two years earlier. During the Second World War Reichers's experiences as a test pilot and long-distance flyer would prove valuable to the Allied forces. As a reserve pilot with the Army Air Corps, he was called up in 1941 to ferry bombers across the North Atlantic to England. The ferrying of aircraft by air from US factories to airfields in Great Britain had begun a year earlier, but in the fall of 1941 American commanders ordered a secret mission to determine the viability of establishing potential air routes across the Pacific Ocean.

On September 29 a B-24 Liberator bomber piloted by Reichers and Major Alva Harvey took off from the newly built Gander airport in central Newfoundland, with a crew consisting of personnel from the Army Air Corps and Pan American Airways. After landing at Prestwick Airport in Scotland, the Liberator continued on to Moscow and from there to airfields along the Pacific rim. The crew surveyed landing fields and assessed whether they would be capable of handling the large aircraft that would be needed in the event of a war with Japan. Reichers and Harvey returned to Washington DC on October 30, six weeks prior to the attack on Pearl Harbour. Reichers was then promoted to colonel and commanded the engineering section of Air Transport Command, which oversaw aircraft ferry operations for the US forces.

S.S. "PRESIDENT ROOSEVELT" & S.S. "PRESIDENT HARDING." SISTER SHIPS. UNITED STATES LINES.

Brushes with death, such as those experienced by Reichers and Rody, were commonplace among pilots during the early decades of aviation. Most crashes were the result of poor pilot training, primitive navigational aids, and notoriously unreliable equipment.

Few pilots could count on the luck of James Mattern, an ambitious Texan who came close to losing his life in the Siberian Arctic. As a teenager, Mattern attended high school in Canada, at Calgary. Later, he spent several years in the US Army Air Corps before becoming an air racer and endurance flyer. In 1932 he prepared to better the round-the-world record of eight days set a year earlier by Wiley Post and Howard Gatty in the *Winnie Mae*. Another former Air Corps pilot, Bennett Griffin, agreed to be Mattern's co-pilot, and a pair of Oklahoma oilmen financed the flight.

Like Post and Amelia Earhart, Mattern and Griffin flew a single-engine Lockheed Vega. The plane, painted red, white, and blue, was named *Century of Progress*, in honour of the Chicago World's Fair which would take place in 1933. The fair, with its slogan "A Century of Progress", celebrated the achievements of science and industry.

On July 5, 1932, Mattern and Griffin took off from Floyd Bennett Field, New York, on their world flight. Their first stop was Harbour Grace, but, as they flew over Newfoundland, the pilots became lost in a fog bank. When the fog cleared, they were flying over Cape Freels, a community on the coast of Bonavista Bay. Completely lost, the pilots wrote a note and dropped it to onlookers, asking for directions to Harbour Grace. Townspeople pointed them in the right direction, and four hours later they finally discovered the Harbour Grace airfield.

After a two-hour refuelling stop, they took off again and flew directly to Berlin, rather than to Ireland or England as other flyers had done. This decision put them three hours ahead of the record time set by the *Winnie Mae*. Mattern and Griffin left for Moscow the next morning, and by now they were confident that the *Century of Progress* would smash the world flight record.

At this point, however, their luck ran out. The plane's engine failed over the Ukraine, forcing the pilots to land, but what they presumed was solid turf turned out to be a peat bog. The landing gear sank, pitching the nose of the plane forward and into the ground. Mattern and Griffin were only slightly injured, but the plane had been badly damaged. The men were listed as missing for two days, until Soviet officials disclosed that they had crashed at Borisov, a town near Minsk.

Despite this setback, Mattern refused to give up. On June 3, 1933, he again took off from Floyd Bennett Field — solo this time — flying the *Century of Progress* on another round-the-world flight. He planned to stop at Chicago towards the end of the journey to celebrate the world's fair. Rather than refuelling in Newfoundland, he continued non-stop to Europe. Nothing was heard from the *Century of Progress* until word came the next day that Mattern had become lost and had landed on a rocky beach in Norway. Although Mattern had lost valuable time, he still managed to reach Moscow several hours ahead of the mark set by the *Winnie Mae* in its 1931 flight.

But Mattern's troubles were only beginning, since mechanical problems continued to plague the *Century of Progress* as it flew across the Soviet Union. On June 14 Mattern took off from Siberia for the last time and headed for Nome, Alaska. He never arrived. As the days — and then weeks — passed, hope faded. He was presumed dead until news broke, on July 7, that he was alive, after being missing for twenty-three days.

His story of those three weeks was one of pain, loneliness, and determination. But it was also a tale of generosity and caring from those who saved his life. The *Century of Progress* had flown without trouble for several hours after taking off from the city of Khabarovsk and flying along the Sea of Okhostk. But the weather deteriorated, so Mattern flew inland along the Anadyr River Valley. He decided to land at the town of Anadyr, before heading over the Bering Sea to Alaska.

Suddenly the oil level dropped, the engine began overheating, and Mattern was forced to land on the rocky tundra. As its landing gear struck the ground, the plane catapulted forward, smashing a wing and crushing the fuselage.

Mattern lay trapped in the cockpit for twenty-four hours, nursing a badly twisted ankle and bruises. Finally, he summoned the strength to smash a hole through the cabin with an axe. He lived in the rear of the plane for another eight days, with only eight chocolate bars to sustain him.

Once his rations had been eaten Mattern decided to walk to the Anadyr River, where he hoped a boat might pass by and rescue him. Carrying a rifle and fishing tackle, he hobbled to the river — his ankle throbbing in agony. On his second day at the river Mattern saw two boats. He fired several shots, but nobody noticed.

The cold was excruciating, so he attempted to build a shelter. Using spruce boughs, he managed to build a small makeshift tent, but it failed to keep the wind out. So Mattern abandoned it and, with great effort, chipped a hole in a nearby glacier, crawled into the cavity and slept.

He then decided that the best place to be noticed was on an island in the middle of the river. So he built a raft, but it flipped over — tossing him into the water. After struggling back to the riverbank, he started a large fire. Mattern recalled:

> When I took off my flying suit, my underclothing, which had been soaked with gasoline from the crash, caught fire, and I had to jump back into the icy river.

A second attempt at building a raft proved much more successful; he got to the island and waited for help — his strength sapped. It was then that a group of Inuit men found Mattern; they took him to their camp, where he was nursed back to health.

For the next week Mattern observed the lives of the nomadic families who tended to him. He observed their work, entertainment, and rituals. Mattern wrote in the *New York Times*:

A caribou-killing ceremony and feast were held. After the feast the tent was darkened. It was already smoke-filled. A drum was produced, and we sat there for five hours, listening to the same monotonous beat and to the cries of the natives until they had worked themselves almost into hysterics.

A few men then agreed to take him by boat to the town of Anadyr. "For the next two days every stroke of the oars sang out the grand old word – 'America'," he wrote.

Mattern remained in Anadyr for more than a week, until the Soviet government could find a plane to fly him to Nome, Alaska. However, bad luck would continue to dog Mattern during his return trip to the US. First, the Soviet Sikorsky flying boat ran out of fuel before reaching land, six kilometres from Alaska – Mattern and some of the crew were compelled to row ashore in a rubber raft. He was flown to Fairbanks, and then to several small towns in British Columbia. Another pilot flew him east, with Mattern planning to fly solo to New York from Toronto. But the plane was forced to make a crash landing in northern Ontario, so he abandoned flying altogether and continued his journey by car to Toronto. He finally arrived at the Floyd Bennett Field in a borrowed plane on July 30.

By then, Mattern had been largely forgotten, as Wiley Post had stolen the headlines once again. During Mattern's struggle for survival in Siberia, Post had

Opposite: A crowd gathers in Harbour Grace as James Mattern and Bennett Griffin prepare to cross the Atlantic. Opposite right: The World's Fair was celebrated by the US Postal Service, which produced specially stamped envelopes for the event.

thrilled the American public by breaking his own
record for flying around the world.

In 1932, the year Mattern made his first attempt at circumnavigating the globe, another
would-be hero was planning his own transatlantic heroics. When Stanislaus Hausner embarked
upon his solo flight across the Atlantic in 1932,
he expected to become the first person to fly non-
stop to Warsaw, Poland, from New York. Instead,
Hausner would set a different kind of record —
for time spent marooned at sea in a downed aircraft.

Hausner was a native of Poland who, as a child,
moved to New Jersey with his parents. Being
deeply religious, he joined a Catholic monastic
order. He resigned the order in 1920 and worked for several years as a motion
picture film operator. He also fell in love with aviation, and in 1929 he became
a pilot.

In 1932, despite having little experience as an aviator, Hausner decided to honour the nation of his birth by making a non-stop flight to Warsaw. He acquired a

The Century of Progress,
named in honour of the 1933
Chicago World's Fair, flying
over New York City.

Martha Hausner bids farewell to her husband, Stanislaus, as he departed New York on a solo attempt at reaching Warsaw, Poland. Hausner was forced to ditch his plane in the ocean, and waited eight days to be rescued.

Bellanca-manufactured monoplane and named it *Santa Rosa Maria.*

Despite the mounting death toll among aviators who had attempted to fly across the Atlantic, he did not seem to fully appreciate the dangers. In late May 1932 he took off from Floyd Bennett Field, New York, and hoped to reach Europe within twenty-four hours. But Hausner did not heed the forecasts of poor weather over the Atlantic. After battling fog and cloudy conditions for six hours, he turned around and landed safely in New York.

On June 3, he tried again, even though weather forecasts showed dense fog and low temperatures east of Newfoundland. At the airport that morning, his wife, Martha, helped him stow provisions — ham and chicken sandwiches, oranges, apples, coffee, and water.

"Well, I guess it's time to go," he said, before kissing Martha and taking off. She and Father Paul Knappek of St Casimir Roman Catholic Church in Newark, New Jersey, followed the *Santa Rosa Maria* in another aircraft. After accompanying Hausner for an hour, Martha and Father Knappek returned to Newark; they went immediately to church and prayed.

Hausner would soon need all the help — divine or otherwise — he could muster, although the first leg of the journey passed with relative ease. After twelve hours of flight, the *Santa Rosa Maria* was seen over McCallum, a community on Newfoundland's south coast. But as he continued flying east, the aviator ran into an intense low-pressure weather system. Strong winds slowed the plane and dense fog impaired navigation. Airports in Ireland, England, and Poland were put on alert for the plane, but nothing was seen of it. As the days passed, practically all hope was lost for Hausner's survival. Only his immediate family and Father Knappek had faith that he remained alive.

Their confidence was rewarded on June 11, eight days after Hausner had departed on his transatlantic journey. A British oil tanker, the *Circe Shell*, had plucked the pilot from his partially submerged aircraft. It was floating, tail up, 640 kilometres northeast of the Azores. "There, I told you he was too good a pilot to have been killed," Martha Hausner joyfully told the newspapers.

Upon being rescued, Hausner was suffering from exhaustion, hunger, and dehydration, but he had fully recovered by the time the *Circe Shell* reached Miami, Florida, on June 22. The plane was salvaged by another ship a month later. Even though he had not come close to achieving his goal, Hausner became a hero to many Polish Americans. A parade was held for him in Newark, and large crowds greeted him at several official receptions.

Despite intense public interest in his tale of survival, he refused to discuss his ordeal with the newspapers. He simply reported that fifteen ships had passed by before he was finally rescued. Hausner intended to write a book based upon a diary he had kept while clinging to his stricken aircraft.

But fate would intervene before Hausner could complete his book. In 1935, he was ready to make another attempt at flying to Warsaw, this time starting from Detroit, Michigan. A group of Polish Americans from Detroit had raised money to purchase an aircraft, which was named *Marshall Pilsudski* in honour of a visit to the US by Polish President Jozef Pilsudski.

On May 18, 1935, one month before Hausner expected to fly across the Atlantic, he took off from Detroit's Wayne County Airport, flying over an outdoor mass being held for Pilsudski at Sweetest Heart of Mary Roman Catholic Church in Detroit.

As Hausner circled over the congregation, a wing suddenly sheared away from the aircraft. More than 6,000 people watched and screamed in horror as the plane plunged earthward. It exploded into a fireball upon plowing into the backyard of a home. A priest who witnessed the event recalled:

Hausner was circling high overhead, with the belfry of the church as the centre of the spirals. He apparently made a power dive to gain impetus, and as he came out of it, I saw the right wing crumple off against the sky. The plane dropped like a plummet. There was a muffled explosion and a bright flash of flame. By the time I had run to the scene the plane was almost completely consumed by fire.

A bugler, who had viewed the accident from the church steps, played taps as smoke billowed from the wreckage.

Such dramatic stories of triumph and failure among the aviation fraternity filled newspapers and newsreels of the post-First World War years, but few used the media to promote their activities as successfully as "The Flying Family",

Above left: Kathryn (left) and Janet Lee Hutchinson (right) received much of their schooling in the skies over North America. They, together with their mother, Blanche (centre) and father George, comprised "The Flying Family".

Above Right: "The Flying Family" had become highly popular by the time they embarked upon a transatlantic attempt in 1932. The crew and passengers included (seated from left) film director Norman Alley, and the Hutchinsons: George, Janet Lee, Blanche, and Kathryn. Standing (from left): navigator Peter Redpath, engineer Joseph Ruff, and radio operator Jerry Altfilisch.

whose adventures captivated radio listeners in the early 1930s. The escapades of George and Blanche Hutchinson and their two young daughters, Janet Lee and Kathryn, provided them with a steady income for several years during the Great Depression. However, one of the Hutchinson family's adventures would end with a desperate struggle for survival on the desolate, rugged coast of Greenland.

The family was led by George, who harboured two passions: gambling and aircraft. In the mid-1920s, after winning $8,000 from betting on a horse race, he purchased his first plane, and then learned how to fly. He managed — and subsequently purchased — an airport, and earned money by flying passengers on short excursions. For Hutchinson, aviation became an obsession. Janet Lee Hutchinson recalled:

> [Flying] became a disease; it's all he could think about.

The Hutchinsons first attracted public attention in 1929 when George and his brother Leonard flew with Blanche and the girls in an Army biplane. This stunt marked the beginning of a lucrative flying career for the family, which would end with the outbreak of war in 1939. In 1931 "The Flying Family" embarked on an air tour of all forty-eight states in the US mainland, making regular radio broadcasts throughout their journey. The purpose of this, and their transatlantic attempt a year later, the daughters said, was to prove that air travel was not the preserve of the brave or the rich. Kathryn Hutchinson said:

> Lindbergh was pushing flying the mail, and he thought that was the greatest asset of aviation. Daddy saw this as being secondary to getting people — families — to accepting aviation as a means of transportation. That's why he took the family with him.

With the backing of US President Herbert Hoover, the Hutchinsons succeeded in visiting each of the forty-eight states. At each stop they delighted spectators with their mascot, a lion cub named Governor, in honour of New York Governor Franklin D. Roosevelt, who joined Hoover in supporting their efforts. The family's progress was closely followed by hundreds of thousands of Americans, many of whom listened to their radio broadcasts and telephoned to receive a commemorative jigsaw puzzle offered by the Hutchinsons. Kathryn, who was seven years old at the time, remembered:

> We were on the radio — people called in and got pieces of [a special] jigsaw puzzle. Over a million people phoned in.

Throughout the journey, George and Blanche kept the girls busy by looking out for landmarks. Kathryn said:

> You flew down low and read the name of the town on the railroad station or the water tower — there were no accurate maps available. Daddy would say, "This is what you're going to look for." He'd tell us the letters and we'd go down lower and find out where we were.

Their only mishap occurred when George opted to cross into British Columbia from Oregon to avoid bad weather. But instead of missing the storm, they flew straight into it while crossing over the Rocky Mountains. The aircraft crash-landed, forcing the family to delay completion of the tour until repairs had been made.

Despite this accident, the family's cross-country tour had been a success. Emboldened by the accolades, George and Blanche decided to attempt an even more ambitious project: crossing the Atlantic Ocean. Using a newly purchased twin-engine Sikorsky aircraft, the family took off from Floyd Bennett Field, New York, on August 23, 1932 — Kathryn and Janet Lee were eight and six years old at the time. The plane was named *City of Richmond*, after Richmond, Virginia, where George had spent much of his childhood. Joining the Hutchinsons were three crewmen and a passenger: Canadian navigator Peter Redpath, mechanic Joseph Ruff, radio operator Jerry Altfilisch, and film director Norman Alley.

The eight adventurers landed first in Saint John, New Brunswick, where the aircraft's wheels were replaced with pontoons. The following day they flew to Port Menier, a resort community on Anticosti Island in the Gulf of St Lawrence. Here, they stayed at a luxurious hunting lodge overlooking the St Lawrence River. On August 30, after waiting several days for a favourable weather forecast, they left Anticosti Island. The aircraft cruised north along the coast of Quebec and Labrador, before reaching the community of Hopedale. In his book, *The Flying Family in Greenland*, George Hutchinson describes their arrival:

From the air we could make out the red-and-white building belonging to the Hudson's Bay Company, and used as a general store. Close by we saw the yellow [Moravian] mission house, the church, and the radio station with its two high towers. Looking more closely as we swooped down, we saw many husky dogs lying outside on the ground, among the dilapidated, unpainted wooden huts.

As we circled the village it suddenly came to life. Out of doors popped Eskimos of all ages, and came running down to the water's edge, with the dogs barking and running in all directions. The Eskimos grabbed our hands and shook them in a gesture of welcome, while wide smiles spread across their faces.

• •

Kayakers get a close look at the City of Richmond, *upon its arrival in Hopedale, Labrador.*

• •

The visitors stayed at the Moravian missionary residence, home to Reverend Walter Perret and his family. Hutchinson described the poverty of the Inuit in the community, and criticised the Moravians for encouraging the Inuit to rely upon the missionaries for food, clothing, and medical care:

> Perritt [sic] told us of the work of the Moravian mission, in providing for and educating the Eskimos. We all listened attentively to him of how poor [the Inuit] were in Hopedale. But all this has come about since the white man has attempted to civilise the native. He has made the Eskimo dependent.

On September 2 the visitors took off for Greenland, arriving in Godthaab on the west coast of the Danish territory. But when the *City of Richmond* arrived, the Hutchinsons were surprised by the government's hostile reaction to them — this was not the warm welcome they had become accustomed to in their travels. Denmark, which administered Greenland, refused to grant them landing rights in the territory, even though permits were given to the Hutchinsons to stop in two other Danish dependencies, Iceland and the Faroe Islands.

The Hutchinsons were fined the equivalent of $180. More importantly, they were also compelled to change course; rather than fly to the east coast town of Angmagsalik by crossing the Greenland ice cap — a journey of 740 kilometres — they were ordered to follow the coastline, a distance of almost 2,000 kilometres. The authorities reasoned that the coastal route was safer than flying overland, an argument George Hutchinson dismissed. The order would have dire consequences for the Hutchinsons and their crew.

After a delay of several days, the *City of Richmond* left Godthaab. The plane reached the coastal town of Julianehab, near the southernmost point in Greenland. Here, they waited for favourable weather before leaving for Angmagsalik.

They departed on September 11, but the *City of Richmond* never arrived in Angmagsalik. As the plane neared the community, ice built up along its wings as it flew through dense cloud cover. Thickening ice forced the plane into a slow but inexorable descent, and the crew had no choice but to land in the ocean. Altfilisch, the radio operator, managed to send out an SOS before water swamped the batteries and cut electricity.

The plane taxied to a small island, just fifty-five kilometres from Angmagsalik. Passengers and crew hastily unloaded food, clothing, guns, cushions, tools, and the radio. They also tore a large section of canvas from the wings to build a shelter. As they worked, waves pounded relentlessly against the aircraft. In his book, Hutchinson described the final moments of the *City of Richmond*:

Two 'bergs were gradually drifting closer and closer to the plane as we worked. I don't know exactly how long we worked, but I was the last on board, when I felt the vessel shudder and begin to crumble. I jumped ashore, and we all stood there helplessly, watching the two remorseless icebergs crush the *City of Richmond* between them, and pull this fine, sturdy 'plane under the waters of the cold Atlantic.

The castaways built a makeshift shelter by pulling the canvas between several large rocks. Inside, they laid out rugs and cushions, and in a corner built a rock fireplace. With no trees on the island, they lighted cans of grease to heat themselves and the food supplies taken from the plane. They cooked a seventeen-kilogram lamb that the Hutchinsons had intended to deliver to the governor of Angmagsalik as a gift from the governor of Julianehab. "We used these big cans of lubricant and had greased smoked lamb," Kathryn Hutchinson recalled.

In his account, George described the ordeal as being little more than an adventure. Reality, however, was far different. Altfilisch managed to get the radio working to receive messages, but he was unable to broadcast. The group huddled inside the makeshift shelter, listening helplessly to radio messages from search vessels. Kathryn said:

I wasn't sad or nervous until I saw Daddy crying. We could hear on the radio that they were looking for us, but they weren't really headed in the right direction.

Two days after being marooned, and with the fuel supply running out, the crew of a British fishing trawler, the *Lord Talbott*, spotted their fire. Using the vessel's lights, a Morse code message was sent to the island, asking them to build a second fire if they were indeed the Hutchinson family. Kathryn remembered:

By then we had used all of the grease except for this last can that was going. We had to light something. One of the men [Norman Alley] was a photographer who was taking movies. The film was all we had left to burn. That was really too bad.

As the precious visual account of their journey flared into the night sky, the trawler sent a smaller boat to rescue the Hutchinsons and their crew. Despite the ordeal, the Hutchinsons continued their journey, travelling with the *Lord Talbott* to Iceland and Scotland. A parade was held in their honour in Edinbugh, and they were fêted in London.

Joseph Kennedy, US ambassador to Great Britain, invited them to a reception at his residence — an honour George Hutchinson rebuffed. Kathryn said:

He wouldn't go because he didn't approve of Joe Kennedy. He started his fortune with bootlegging. Daddy was dead set against alcohol.

"The Flying Family" returned home by ship. Seven years later, in 1939, they set off on another ambitious flight — to visit every nation in the world. This was a goodwill mission, designed to promote peace, and they brought with them a scroll which was to be signed by leaders from each country.

They reached every nation in North America, South America, and the West Indies. By then, however, war had broken out in Europe, and the Hutchinsons were forced to halt their tour.

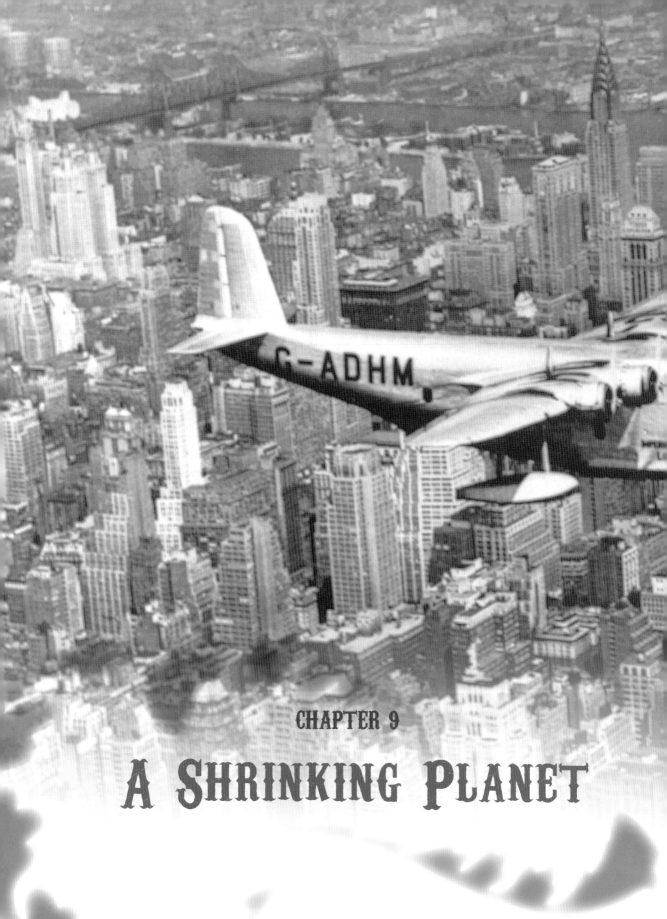

CHAPTER 9

A SHRINKING PLANET

CALEDONIA

By 1938, the wild, youthful years of aviation had almost come to a close. Two events — a new round-the-world speed record, and stringent government regulation of aircraft and pilots — marked the beginning of a new era, one where members of the general public could buy a ticket and fly almost anywhere in the world.

It was perhaps fitting that Howard Hughes would end the pioneer phase of flight. Although he had inherited a drilling tool company, Hughes demonstrated little interest in the firm; instead the eccentric millionaire sustained a life-long obsession with flight. Hughes used the profits earned by his businesses to feed his love for aviation, as well as his other passions, principally motion pictures and beautiful film starlets. These three interests sometimes converged; as a movie producer he

Millionaire and legendary eccentric, Howard Hughes, was obsessed with flight. In 1938, he smashed the round-the-world record set by Wiley Post.

released *Hell's Angels*, a 1930 film portraying aerial battles of the First World War. The production, which starred Jean Harlow, became the first multi-million-dollar movie, costing Hughes $3.8 million. Hughes, who also directed the film when the original director resigned, hired former First World War pilots to fly stunt planes, three of whom died while flying battle scenes.

But Hughes was also an avid pilot, and he revelled in setting speed records. Although he was enormously wealthy and could easily hire pilots for dangerous flights, Hughes insisted on personally test-flying new aircraft — a dangerous occupation at a time when aeronautical engineering was in its infancy. Hughes was badly injured on one occasion when the prototype of a plane, the XF-11, which was designed and built by his company, malfunctioned during a test flight and crashed.

Like many early aviators, most notably Charles Lindbergh, Hughes also played a central role in designing aircraft he flew. Despite having no formal education as an engineer, Hughes improvised in order to boost the speed and efficiency of his planes. In 1935, he set a US coast-to-coast speed record in a new aircraft, the H-1. This prototype would influence the design of Second World War fighter planes, with its drooping ailerons, split flaps, hydraulic landing gear, fire-suppression system, and movable pilot's seat.

In 1938, he decided to smash the record for flying around the world, which was set five years earlier by Wiley Post. Hughes reputedly spent approximately $300,000 financing the venture, which included buying a specially built Lockheed twin-engine aircraft. He named the plane *New York World's Fair 1939* in order to promote ticket sales for the event.

But there was a second reason for the urgency of this flight. Despite Hughes's bravado, time was rapidly running out for the free-spirited men and women who rode their machines into the skies. In February 1938, legislation had been introduced to the US House of Representatives that would establish an independent agency with greater authority than the Commerce Department's Bureau of Air Commerce, which was then responsible for regulating air traffic. Among its powers, the new organization would certify pilots, aircraft, and airfields. More importantly to Hughes, it might also ban so-called stunt flights.

By June the new regulatory agency, the Civil Aeronautics Authority, had been approved by Congress and was signed into law by the president; however, it would not actually take effect until early August.

The Civil Aeronautics Authority would soon have the ability to disallow Hughes's world flight, so he dedicated himself to completing the journey before its regulations came into effect. On July 10, the *New York World's Fair 1939* took off from Floyd Bennett Field in New York. Besides Hughes, the aircraft held a crew of four men. One of his co-pilots was Harry Connor, who had flown across the Atlantic Ocean with Canadian Erroll Boyd in 1930. Other crewmen included co-pilot and navigator Thomas Thurlow, engineer Edward Lund, and radio technician Richard Stoddart.

Poor weather over waters east of Newfoundland slowed their progress across the Atlantic and Hughes worried that the plane might run out of fuel before reaching Europe; so to reduce consumption the crew was forced to reduce air speed. Despite slowing down, however, the aircraft reached Paris in sixteen hours, thirty-five minutes – half the time Lindbergh took in 1927.

The record-setting pace then continued unabated as Hughes flew across Europe, the Soviet Union, and then back to North America. When Hughes returned to Floyd Bennett Field on July 14, his time of three days and nineteen hours had halved Post's record.

A crowd of 20,000 people mobbed the reclusive millionaire as he stepped from the plane. The next day an estimated 1.5 million people lined the streets of New York in a tickertape parade held to honour his achievement. When the festivities ended, sanitation workers had to clean 1,800 tonnes of rubbish from the streets.

The Lockheed Super Electra piloted by Howard Hughes above Manhattan on a test run prior to his round-the-world flight in 1938.

Perhaps wisely, in light of the new aviation laws coming into effect, Hughes refused to take full credit for the achievement. Instead, he characterised the flight as a work of engineering prowess, rather than a successful conclusion to a risky adventure. This assessment was supported by the newly minted Civil Aeronautics Authority, whose members belated offered official congratulations to Hughes for his "most effective demonstration possible of the contribution that scientific preparation and organization can make to safety and speed in the air."

One of Hughes's most important contributions to aviation would be the creation of a passenger airline, Trans World Airlines, which began competing for American and transatlantic passenger traffic starting in the 1940s. Hughes's legacy would continue well beyond his death in 1978. Hughes Aircraft Company, which had been established in 1935, became a world leader in high technology systems for scientific, military, and global applications. Raytheon Company acquired the firm in 1998.

Although Hughes's round-the-world flight in 1938 was widely acclaimed, his achievement that year was almost obscured by another aviator whose exploits also garnered newspaper headlines. Douglas Corrigan was a pilot and mechanic who, while working for Ryan Aeronoautical Company, helped build and modify the plane Lindbergh used to win the New York to Paris race in 1927.

In the early 1930s, Corrigan bought a Curtiss Robin, a small one-engine plane which he named *Sunshine*, from the Curtiss-Robin Aircraft Company, with the intention of emulating Lindbergh's transatlantic flight. However, the Bureau of Air Commerce had repeatedly denied his application to fly across the Atlantic, even though Corrigan had installed a more powerful engine and additional fuel tanks into his plane.

But Corrigan was determined to make the journey, so in July 1938 he flew from California to Floyd Bennett Field where Hughes's plane was also being readied. During his cross-continent flight, a fuel leak had occurred, but Corrigan was worried that the authorities would ground him if he waited to make repairs. So on July 17 he took off in his damaged plane with the intention of reaching Ireland, although Corrigan officially logged Long Beach, California, as his destination.

During the flight, fuel leaked into the cabin, forcing Corrigan to puncture the cockpit floor with a screwdriver in order to allow for drainage away from the hot exhaust pipe. Despite the leak, Corrigan arrived safely at Baldonnel Aerodrome in Dublin after a twenty-eight-hour flight. American authorities responded by suspending his pilot's licence for fourteen days, a mild punishment that Corrigan happily accepted.

He was then dubbed "Wrong Way Corrigan", and upon his return to New York was given a tumultuous welcome from the public. He wrote a book about his exploits, starred in his own film biography, and endorsed numerous "wrong way" products. Corrigan tested bombers during the Second World War and flew aircraft to Europe for the Ferry Command.

Hughes's round-the-world flight in 1938, along with Corrigan's triumph, marked an end to the pioneering era of flight. The aviation industry was maturing, with airline companies establishing passenger and airmail routes across North America and within Europe. In addition, large flying boats were beginning to prove their reliability over the world's oceans.

People were clamouring to experience the convenience of flight for themselves, and less interested in following the aerial feats of intrepid pilots. But this did not stop two more adventurers from trying their luck in crossing the Atlantic prior to the advent of the Second World War. Their experiences demonstrated that ocean flights were still dangerous for aviators and could claim the lives of the unprepared and the unlucky.

The newly built Gander airport in central Newfoundland unexpectedly received

A Pan American World Airways flying boat, the Clipper III, *at Botwood in 1937, proving that transatlantic passenger flights were close to reality. The aircraft is shown being serviced (next page).*

its first aircraft from outside Newfoundland in May 1939 when Carl Backman arrived from Bangor, Maine. Backman, a pilot of Swedish heritage, was planning to fly non-stop to Stockholm; however, American regulations effectively banned transatlantic flights by small aircraft like his. To circumvent the rules, Backman found a loophole — he claimed to have sold his plane to a Swedish buyer and alleged that he was merely delivering the craft to Sweden. The ninety-horsepower, single-engine monoplane carried no radio, and Backman brought only sandwiches and a thermos of tea with him as he took off from Gander on May 15, bound for Sweden. He was never seen again.

On May 28, another lone flyer, Thomas Smith, took to the air from Old Orchard Beach, Maine, in a small plane, an American-made Aeronca 65-C, which he named *Baby Clipper*. Fully loaded, the aircraft weighed just 860 kilograms. Smith, who claimed to be using the flight to demonstrate the practicality of using light planes for long-distance flights, expected to reach England within two days. The *New York Times* reported that Smith had spent just $30 on fuel for the entire 4,800-kilometre journey.

Like Backman, Smith did not bring a radio for the flight, although he carried a first-aid kit, a revolver, and mosquito netting in case the plane was forced down over land. After taking off, Smith disappeared. His fate remained unknown until 1941, when a Canadian Air Force patrol aircraft discovered wreckage of the *Baby Clipper* near Burgeo on Newfoundland's south coast. Smith's body was never found, but inside the cockpit was a note written by him, which indicated that he survived the crash and had attempted to walk to safety:

Have some food and emergency supplies. I'm walking South, then will walk west if I hit ocean. North-Northwest. That is down the mountain. If I can't find a house will try to come back to ship. Weather sleeting — Thermometer dropping — Am afraid to stay in ship for fear of freezing while asleep.

In a rare partnership between rival airlines, Imperial Airways and Pan American conducted joint test flights of their flying boats on the treacherous North Atlantic route. Imperial had to strip the Caledonia (seen here in Botwood) of all non-essential equipment in order to fly non-stop across the ocean in 1937.

A refuelling barge (above) and flying boat station (opposite) were built at Botwood by Pan American and Imperial Airways. Similar facilities had also been installed in England, Ireland, New Brunswick, and Quebec.

While the short-lived age of air racing was coming to a close, a new era of commercial aviation was already maturing. Airline companies were now looking to bridge the world's oceans, this time using planes rather than airships such as the *Graf Zeppelin*.

On July 5, 1937, a group of spectators watched in awe from Botwood, a town on Newfoundland's northwest coast, as a huge, four-engine Pan American World Airways flying boat skimmed along the water and lumbered into the sky. The Sikorsky S-42B, named *Clipper III*, was leaving Botwood and heading towards the port of Foynes in County Limerick, Ireland. Unlike previous transatlantic attempts, this flight was not being conducted by a group of thrill-seekers and there would be no cash reward or tickertape parade waiting for Captain Harold Gray and his three crewmen.

Instead, this was a rare collaboration between two rival airlines, Pan American and Britain's Imperial Airways. They were hoping to establish commercial transatlantic

air services linking Britain, Ireland, Newfoundland, Canada, and the United States. When the *Clipper III* disappeared over the horizon, the dignitaries visiting Botwood for the event did not immediately climb aboard a train and return to their homes. Instead, they waited in anxious anticipation for the second partner in this unique transatlantic experiment.

They would not be disappointed. The next morning, July 6, another aircraft appeared on the horizon. With its engines roaring, an Imperial Airways flying boat, a Short Empire Class craft named *Caledonia*, landed in the calm bay and cruised towards land. It had taken the aircraft sixteen hours to fly to Botwood from Ireland.

Waiting on shore to greet Captain Arthur Wilcockson and his three crewmen was Newfoundland's governor Humphrey Walwyn who had travelled from St John's to watch the two aircraft achieve this milestone in aviation history. By the time the *Caledonia* had reached its destination, the *Clipper III* had already arrived safely at Foynes.

The *Caledonia* then flew to Montreal on July 8 and completed its journey by arriving in New York the next day. It made a return flight to Ireland a week later. The *Clipper III*, meanwhile, flew from Foynes to Southampton, England, before returning to New York, via Botwood and Shediac in Canada's eastern province of New Brunswick. Imperial Airways and Pan American aircraft passed through Botwood and Shediac more than a dozen times during this first year of transatlantic flights.

The timing of these trial flights was no accident. Just one year earlier, in 1936, the *Hindenburg* had exploded while landing in New Jersey, a catastrophe that put an end to passenger airships, which at that time offered the only transatlantic air service. Despite the disaster, there was a growing public demand for a fast, convenient form of air travel, and the void left by the German airships provided an opportunity for Pan American and Imperial Airways.

These two companies were in an ideal position to take charge. Several years earlier, in 1933, they had begun planning a transatlantic flying boat service. This collaboration between the airlines also involved the governments of the United States, Canada, Newfoundland, and Britain. Botwood was selected as an operational base following an extensive survey in 1933 by Charles Lindbergh and Anne Morrow Lindbergh, who were hired by Pan American to survey possible landing sites in North America and Europe.

Lindbergh had long believed that land planes would eventually supplant flying boats as the most effective method for crossing the Atlantic, principally because sea bases needed sheltered harbours which were often closed to air traffic by poor weather. Once paved runways became commonplace, Lindbergh expected commercial air carriers to switch to land planes for ocean crossings. But during the 1930s the world's major airlines focused on flying boats, primarily due to the scarcity of paved airfields. Seaplane terminals were also significantly cheaper and faster to build than airports.

Botwood was a logical place to situate a seaplane base, because the community is located at the end of a long, narrow fjord. The waters are generally calm, although sea ice during the winter and spring limited the flying season to only five months of the year. Botwood was already well known to aviators. For several years, beginning in 1920, pilot Sidney Cotton used Botwood as a base for his small planes. In addition to delivering mail to isolated communities, Cotton had been hired to spot seal herds on pack ice during the annual Newfoundland seal hunt.

After winning exclusive rights to use Botwood for transatlantic flights in 1933,

Imperial Airways signed an agreement with Pan American that allowed its US counterpart to share the future seaplane base.

Although flying boats were new to Newfoundland, by 1937 they had become a fairly common form of transportation in many parts of the world. The aircraft were romantically dubbed "clippers of the skies", akin to the swift, sleek clipper sailing vessels of the nineteenth century.

The transatlantic trial flights of 1937 were designed to prove the viability of flying seaplanes across the ocean on a commercial basis. To the public, these initial experiments appeared to be an overwhelming success. But the airlines knew otherwise; in fact the flights proved that improvements in engine power and fuel efficiency were urgently required if their goals of a transatlantic service were to be realised. Existing aircraft were not yet powerful enough to carry heavy loads over long distances without stopping for fuel.

But the dream of commercial transatlantic flights across the Atlantic remained tantalizingly close to being realised. Although Pan American's Sikorsky S-42 flying boats had been built in 1934 especially for long-distance flying, it was becoming clear to the company – just three years later – that the planes were already obsolete. Rather than start commercial transatlantic flights with its Sikorskys, Pan American opted to wait for a new aircraft, which was being designed and built by Boeing. In 1938, Pan American suspended its transatlantic program while Boeing finished fabrication of the first of its new fleet of planes.

As for Imperial Airways, it also faced limitations to its flying boats; in order to fly non-stop across the Atlantic in 1937 the *Caledonia* had been stripped of all unnecessary weight and carried no cargo or passengers. Initially, during the early 1930s, Imperial Airways believed it had a winner with its S-23 Empire Class flying boats, manufactured by Short Brothers. The planes were built to capitalise on a decision by the British government, in the mid-1930s, to transport all first-class mail by air. The S-23s allowed Imperial Airways to operate passenger and airmail flights to locations around the world. This made the flying boats a vital element in linking distant outposts of the British Empire.

The S-23s proved so successful that Imperial Airways ordered forty-two of them. However, the planes could not even match the range of Pan American's fleet of Sikorsky S-42s. But unlike their American rival, which, after the 1937 trial flights, focused on building a plane that could efficiently fly across the Atlantic, Imperial Airways opted to tinker with its S-23s.

In 1938, Imperial Airways tried an innovation called the "piggyback", which featured a Short S-23 flying boat carrying a smaller seaplane. It was dubbed a Short-Mayo Composite, in recognition of its designer, Robert Mayo. The concept was simple: the larger aircraft carried the smaller one part of the way across the Atlantic. Midway across, the seaplane was released to continue the journey to North America, while the transporter returned to base. The piggyback was designed solely to carry airmail across the Atlantic.

The first transatlantic piggyback flight took place on July 20, 1938. Under the command of Arthur Wilcockson, a modified flying boat, named *Maia*, took off from Foynes in Ireland. On its back the transporter carried a four-engine floatplane called *Mercury*. Wilcockson had flown to New York from Foynes on the inaugural transatlantic flight by the *Caledonia* a year earlier.

After several hours flying west over the Atlantic, the *Mercury* was released, whereupon Wilcockson turned the *Maia* around and headed back to Ireland. Because the *Mercury* had used little fuel — except during takeoff — to reach the mid-Atlantic, its pilot, Donald Bennett, was able to fly directly to Montreal with a cargo of 450 kilograms of mail without stopping first in either Botwood

• •

The "piggyback" innovation allowed Imperial Airways to fly airmail non-stop to Montreal from Ireland, as well as on other long routes. The Maia *acted as a booster aircraft for the* Mercury *seaplane by flying it partway out to sea, and then releasing the smaller aircraft so that it could complete the journey.*

• •

or Shediac. The entire journey, from Ireland to Montreal, took just over twenty hours to complete. Although the piggyback experiment had proved successful, it was also cumbersome and expensive. The idea was abandoned after its initial trials that year.

By 1939, Pan American was ready to start commercial passenger and airmail service across both the North and South Atlantic. For this, the airline introduced its new fleet of Boeing 314s, revolutionary aircraft in terms of flying range as well as passenger comfort and safety.

On June 24, 1939, a Boeing 314, named *Yankee Clipper*, took off from New York on the first airmail flight along Pan American's new northern route. Under the command of Harold Gray, it landed at seaplane bases in Shediac, Botwood, and Foynes, before finishing the journey in Southampton, England. Passenger flights commenced the following month. Weekly return flights continued until war broke out in September, whereupon Pan American ceased flying to Southampton for the remainder of 1939 and instead finished the flights in Foynes.

While Pan American was flying both passengers and airmail using the new, advanced Boeing aircraft, Imperial Airways was relegated to using its outdated planes. In order to carry mail across the Atlantic, modifications were made to allow for the mid-air refuelling of two S-23 flying boats. Handley Page Harrow air tankers were located at airports in Gander and Shannon, Ireland, to provide mid-air refuelling. Two flying boats, named *Caribou* and *Cabot*, made sixteen experimental transatlantic flights during August and September 1939 on Imperial Airways' New York-Montreal-Botwood-Foynes-Southampton route.

In the months prior to the outbreak of war in September 1939, two other airlines conducted transatlantic trial flights through Botwood. Air France completed three flights, but ceased further transatlantic activities following the declaration of war. American Export Airlines, a new US airline, made several trial flights using PBY Catalina twin-engine flying boats. American Export planes would become regular visitors to Botwood from 1942 to 1945.

All four airlines had been ready to offer passenger flights across the Atlantic when the Second World War intervened. Suddenly, military prerogatives took precedence over civilian priorities. The immediate effect on Botwood of the war in Europe was a reduction in air traffic; due to official US neutrality Pan American and American Export were forced to cancel their transatlantic flights through Shediac and Botwood after 1939. The British also curtailed

Among those who offered support to US troops during the Second World War was Frank Sinatra (above left). Other dignitaries included Franklin Roosevelt and Winston Churchill (above right).

their transatlantic flights during the first two years of conflict. In 1940, British Overseas Airways Corporation (BOAC), which had been created with the merger of Imperial Airways and British Airways, made eleven Atlantic crossings. The planes, which carried mail and passengers, had been improved since the previous year and were now capable of flying across the Atlantic without mid-air refuelling. BOAC completed eleven further flights in 1941, after acquiring two of the superior Boeing 314 Clippers.

Botwood had become a busy community in 1941; the Royal Canadian Air Force began construction of a seaplane station and army base, thereby boosting the community's population dramatically. Britain's Royal Air Force, which had taken control of the civilian flying boat base, sent personnel to Botwood from the new Gander airport whenever a seaplane was scheduled to arrive. The Botwood base proved useful to the military as well as to civilian airlines during the war. The RCAF conducted anti-submarine patrols from there, mostly using Consolidated PBY Canso flying boats (a Canadian-built version of the Catalina flying boat). Many powerful political and military leaders passed through the town during the war, including Franklin Roosevelt, Prime Minister Winston

Churchill, and Lord Louis Mountbatten.

American Export resumed its transatlantic flying boat service in 1942. Under contract to the US Navy, the airline flew passengers across the Atlantic until the end of the war.

As for Pan American, it had maintained its southern transatlantic flying boat passenger service throughout the early years of war in Europe. Its flying boats flew between New York and Lisbon, Portugal, via Bermuda and the Azores. Pan American resumed passenger service on the northern passenger route to Ireland in 1943, several months after the US declared war on Germany.

Flying boats may have been high-class transportation, but travelling by air was still a relatively dangerous way to travel. Two flying boats were destroyed in accidents at Botwood during the Second World War, killing a total of twenty-one people.

On October 3, 1942, the *Excalibur*, a Sikorsky S-44A operated by American Export, crashed during takeoff, killing all fifteen passengers and crew. Levi Skinner, who was in charge of arrivals and departures at Botwood, recalled the rescue effort:

I shot the boat up alongside the aircraft near the tail section that was afloat, and I could see a man's hand sticking out about three feet [one metre] under water; so I reached down and got a hold of his hand and squeezed it to see if there was any life in it, but there was no sign of life. I pulled on the hand to try and get the body aboard the boat, but the body was stuck in the fold of the plane where it had cracked off. I realised that if I just left the dead body there that it would probably be swept away by the current, so I tied a piece of rope around the wrist and secured it to the plane's fuselage.

A US Army ring, with the name Colonel Whitaker inscribed on the inside, had slid off the dead man's finger and into Skinner's hand. He contacted the family of the dead officer and returned the ring to them. Six more people died on November 8, 1943, when a RCAF Canso flying boat crashed into the water while touching down at Botwood. There were five survivors.

Although the flying boat stations at Foynes and Botwood played important roles during the war, of greater importance to military planners was overcoming the problem of getting land-based warplanes from North America to Europe.

With German forces overwhelming much of Europe throughout 1939-1940, Britain girded itself against invasion by building aircraft capable of attacking enemy ships and troop carriers, as well as to counter the bombers that were pulverizing English cities and industrial infrastructure. In addition, Britain needed to bolster its own bomber squadrons in order to mount attacks on German rail lines and factories.

British industry could not build planes quickly enough to match the Germans; so the United States, although being officially neutral, began supplying Britain with aircraft — initially Lockheed-made Hudson bombers — soon after the war began. During the initial months, newly manufactured planes had to be towed over the Canadian border at North Dakota in order to ensure that the US adhered to its strict neutrality laws. The planes were then flown to eastern Canada and transported by ship across the Atlantic.

When hostilities began, British wartime planners had discounted the idea of flying bombers directly from North America, via Newfoundland, to Europe for several reasons: a lack of proper airport infrastructure in Newfoundland, a shortage of trained air navigators, the possibility of attacks on bombers as they were being flown overseas, and concerns about flying aircraft over the harsh North Atlantic — particularly during the notoriously treacherous winter months.

By the summer of 1940, manufacturers had orders for 26,000 aircraft. However, sending such a large numbers of planes by ship to Britain from Canada was fraught with difficulty due to German U-boat predations on merchant ships. Time was also an important consideration; the British were reeling from German successes in continental Europe, and without a faster method of transporting new planes the English faced the possibility of having insufficient equipment to counter an invasion.

Therefore, in mid-1940 Britain's Minister of Aircraft Production, Canadian-born Lord Beaverbrook, decided to test the feasibility of transporting bombers to Britain from North America by air.

The viability of flying newly built warplanes from North American territories to Great Britain was proven in November 1940, when seven Hudson bombers flew non-stop from Gander, Newfoundland to Aldergrove airport in Northern Ireland.

In November 1940, a group of seven Hudson bombers, led by Captain Donald Bennett of the Royal Air Force, left Saint-Hubert airport near Montreal and arrived at the recently built Newfoundland Airport adjacent Gander Lake. The land-based airport had been built following the signing of the 1935 North Atlantic Civil Aviation Agreement. With this pact, Canada, Great Britain, Ireland, and the British-controlled administration in Newfoundland selected suitable locations for constructing new airports along the Atlantic coasts of North America and northern Europe that would be capable of handling flying boats and land-based transatlantic aircraft.

The Gander Lake area had several advantages over other locations in Newfoundland, outstripping even Harbour Grace, which until then had been the favoured refuelling stop for transatlantic aviators. However, not only was Gander Lake free from coastal fog, it was also designated as an alternate landing site for flying boats in the late 1930s when sea conditions were poor at the flying boat terminal in Botwood. On November 10, Bennett and the seven Hudson bombers took off from Gander on an experimental flight, and several hours later all of the aircraft landed safely at Aldergrove Royal Air Force Base, thirty kilometres northwest of Belfast in Northern Ireland. This achievement proved the viability of

non-stop transatlantic flights and would soon lead to the emergence of several military airports in eastern North America, including Dorval west of Montreal and communities in Newfoundland and Labrador.

The Royal Air Force established Ferry Command to coordinate air transport of bombers to Britain, and during the war thousands of newly built planes were flown from North America to Prestwick, Scotland. The pace of the ferrying operations grew even more frenetic after the United States entered the war in late 1941. Soon Britain, Canada and the US were sharing Gander, along with a huge new base in Goose Bay, Labrador, while the Americans established their own trans-atlantic service at a new airport in the town of Stephenville on Newfoundland's west coast.

The success of these ferrying operations led to other routes being established, including one across the southern Atlantic which linked the US to Egypt, using bases in the West Indies, South America, Ascension Island, and Africa.

A B24 bomber, which crashed on Christmas Day in 1943, was one of dozens that met a similar fate at Gander during the Second World War.

Although the vast majority of planes arrived safely in Europe, accidents inevitably claimed dozens of aviators and their machines. The best-known victim was Frederick Banting, co-discoverer of insulin, who died in February 1941 when the Hudson bomber in which he was flying as a passenger crashed shortly after takeoff from Gander en route to Britain.

When the war in Europe ended in May 1945, the need for ferrying large numbers of aircraft to Europe immediately disappeared. Within weeks Gander airport was converted to civilian needs and by year's end several airlines, including Pan American World Airways, Trans-Canada Airlines (later Air Canada), and British Overseas Airway Corporation (later British Airways), were using Gander for transatlantic passenger air service.

Two immediate casualties of peace were the flying boat stations at Botwood and Foynes, both of which quickly closed. The Foynes operation was replaced by nearby Shannon Airport, which was established during the late-1930s to handle transatlantic land-based aircraft.

New airports rendered obsolete almost all flying boats at war's end except in areas of the world where paved airfields were scarce, such as in remote parts Southeast Asia. The last regular passenger service using flying boats ended in 1967.

Today, flying across any of the world's oceans is largely taken for granted, as the jet age has turned air travel into a safe, convenient, and economical way to travel. The passage of time has left only fading memories of that brief era when pilots were heroic figures and whose exploits in the air were closely followed by entire nations.

Air races, whether across continents or over oceans, ceased to attract much attention following the Second World War, as flight became a commonplace activity. By then, the competition between airships and fixed-wing aircraft had been

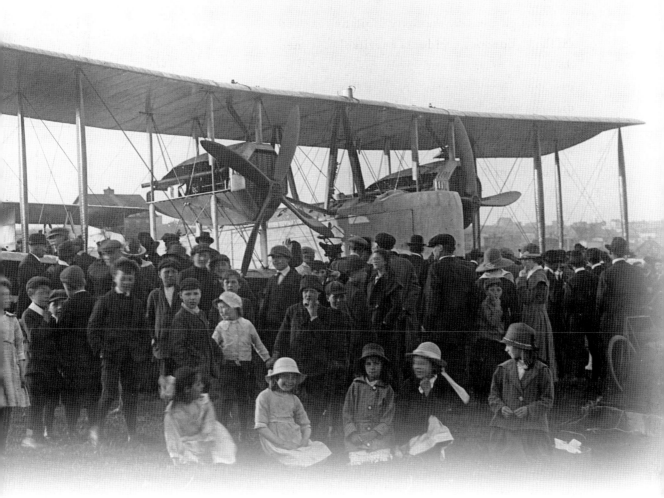

settled, and newspapers were no longer offering cash prizes for being the first to fly between the world's great cities.

It is now difficult to comprehend the degree to which people became enthralled by pioneering pilots and their machines. Undoubtedly, this interest was fuelled by novelty, along with a desire to forget the carnage of the First World War and then the devastation wrought by the Great Depression.

But this is only part of the answer, for surely the men and women who took to the skies were answering the question people throughout the course of history have asked as they gazed at birds soaring above them: "What would it be like to fly?"

Children play in the foreground of the Vickers Vimy bomber in St John's, which was flown across the Atlantic Ocean in 1919 by John Alcock and Arthur Whitten Brown.

IMAGE CREDITS

Key: B Bottom; C Centre; L Left; R Right; T Top
Abbreviations

AP – Associated Press; Byrd – Byrd Polar Research Centre; AMD – Archives and Manuscripts Division Queen Elizabeth II Library, Memorial University; MHA – Maritime History Archive, Memorial University; NYT – New York Times; PANL – The Rooms Provincial Archives Newfoundland and Labrador; SI – Smithsonian Institution.

p1 PANL B21-114; pp2-3 PANL H5-29; pp4-5 SI 80-18073

Chapter 1

pp. 8-9 PANL A12-11; 10B PANL B21-158, 10T AMD 232-3.04; 11 PANL B21-161; 12T SI 90-2211; 12-3 AMD 232-3.05, 13B AMD 232-3.05; 15 Trepassey Historical Society; 16 US Naval Historical Center; 18-9 PANL B21-155; 20 Private Collection; 23T AMD 232-3.09, 23B PANL A47-15; 24 PANL A47-22; 25 PANL A47-28; 26TL *Connacht Tribune* & Irish Newspaper Archive; 26-7 Library of Congress; 31 SI 2004-18936; 32-3 SI-83-390.

Chapter 2

pp. 34-5 AMD 232-3.16; 36BL Sheet Music: Private Collection, 36TR PANL A46-119; 37T MHA, 37B SI 94-2; 39B Corbis, 39T PANL B21-177; 40T PANL B21-175; 42 inset SI 81-3420, 42B Private Collection; 45B Byrd 7744-5, 45T Byrd 7748-1; 46B Private Collection, 46T AMD 232-3.12; 48 AMD 232-3.14; 49 AMD 232-3.15; 50T AMD 232-13.18, 50B PANL A46-98; 53T PANL B21-80, 53B PANL B21-78; 54 AMD 232-3.19; 55 NYT 7 September 1927; 56 PANL A46-8; 57 PANL B21-46; 58-9B Byrd 7739-10; 59T Private Collection; 61 Corbis.

Chapter 3

pp. 62-3 PANL A17-88; 65T NYT 1 September 1927, 65B NYT 25 December 1927; 66 Corbis; 68L Corbis, 68R Central Press; 70L *Anaconda Standard* 18 June 1928, 70R Private Collection; 71 Parson, B. 1983. *The Challenge of the Atlantic.* St John's: Robinson-Blackmore Book Publishers; 74-5 SI 73-4032, 74 inset Trepassey Historical Society; 76 PANL B8-38; 79 Corbis.

Chapter 4

pp. 80-1 Sheet Music: Jack Mills Music Publishers; 84L *Aviation Stories and Mechanics*

BIBLIOGRAPHY

Air Commodore HG Brackley: *Air of Authority — A History of RAF Organization*. www.rafweb. org/Biographies/Brackley.htm.

Allward, M. 1981. *An Illustrated History of Seaplanes and Flying Boats*. Ashbourne, United Kingdom: Dorset Press.

Almond, P. 1997. *Aviation: The Early Years*. Cologne, Germany: Konemann Verlagsgesellschaft.

Amelia Earhart. www.acepilots.com/earhart.html.

Archbold, R. 2005. *Hindenburg: An Illustrated History*. Toronto: Madison Press Books.

Aviation Stories & Mechanics (Summer 1928).

Balbo, I. 1934. *My Air Armada*. London: Hurst and Blackett.

Ball, N.R. (ed.) 1988. B*uilding Canada: A History of Public Works*. Toronto: University of Toronto Press.

Bonds, R. 2003. *A Century of Flight*. London: Salamander Books.

Botwood Heritage Society.

Bowman, B and Parsons, B. 1983. *The Challenge of the Atlantic*. St John's: Robinson-Blackmore.

Browne Papers. Queen Elizabeth II Library, Memorial University.

Byrd, RE. 1928. *Skyward*. New York: GP Putnam's Sons.

Capelotti, PJ. 2002. *Technology and Memory at Port Burwell, 1929*. The Pine Tree Line. www.pinetreeline.org/other/other8/other8cl.html.

Cardoulis, JN. 1990. *A Friendly Invasion: The American Military in Newfoundland* 1940-1990. St John's: Breakwater.

Charles Nungesser. *Legendary Aviators and Aircraft of World War One*. 2003. <http://www. acepilots.com/wwi/fr_nungesser.html>.

Daily News. St John's. September 1927.

Dunmore, S. 2004. *Undaunted*. Toronto: McClelland & Stewart.

Earhart, A. 1932. *The Fun of It: Random Records of My Own Flying and of Women in Aviation*. New York: Brewer, Warren & Putnam.

Elliott, J. May/June 2004. *Profile: Amelia Earhart*. Empowerment4Women.org. <http:// www.empowerment4women.org/respect/mj04_ameliaearhart.html>.

Ellis, FH. 1962. *Canada's Flying Heritage*. Toronto: University of Toronto Press.

Ellis, FH and Ellis, E. 1963. *Atlantic Air Conquest*. London: William Kimber and Company.

Amelia Earhart and the Friendship. Folklore of Trepassey. Trepassey, Newfoundland and Labrador: Trepassey Public Library.

Encyclopedia of Newfoundland and Labrador, Volume I (1981). St John's: Newfoundland Book Publishers (1967) Ltd.

Ethell JL. *Smithsonian Frontiers of Flight*. New York: Crown Publishing Group.

Evening Telegram. St John's. September 1927.

Frances Wilson Grayson. <http://prion.bchs.uh.edu/george/grayson/fwgrayson.htm>.

Heppenheimer, TA. *Hawker Siddely. Essays: Aerospace Industry*. U.S. Centennial of Flight Commission. 2003. <http://www.centennialofflight.gov/essay/Aerospace/Hawker/Aero51a.htm>.

Hutchinson, GR. 1935. *The Flying Family in Greenland*. Binghamton, New York: Thomas Y Crowell Company.

Hamlen, J. 1971. *Flight Fever*. New York: Doubleday & Company.

Hardesty, V. 2002. *Lindbergh: Flight's Enigmatic Hero*. Orlando, Florida: Tehabi Books.

Hawker Siddeley. <http://www.centennial of flight.gov>.

Holt, P. R-34: *An Atlantic Airship Exploit*. Aviation History, 2002. <http://history1900s.about.com/library/prm/blr34atlanticairship5.htm>.

Jablonski, E. 1972. *Atlantic Fever*. Toronto: Collier-Macmillan Canada.

Krippene, BL. 1995. *Wingwalker: From Wisconsin to Norway, The Larson Brothers and Clyde Lee*. Friendship, Wisconsin: New Past Press Inc.

Lindbergh, AM. 1938. *Listen! The Wind*. New York: Harcourt, Brace & World Inc.

Lindbergh, CA. 1953. *The Spirit of St. Louis*. New York: Scribner's Sons.

Lost Adventurers: Daring But Not So Lucky. Pioneers of the Sky. (n.d.). <http://goodies.freeservers.com/lostadventurers.html>.

Luff, D. 1993. *Mollison: The Flying Scotsman*. Washington: Smithsonian Institution Press.

Mackworth-Praed, B. 1990. *Aviation: The Pioneer Years*. London: Studio Editions Ltd.

New York Times. 1927 to 1939.

Newsletter of the Inland Waterways of Ireland. Winter 2001.

Newfoundland Herald. January 2, 1988.

Newfoundland Quarterly. Autumn 1933.

O'Brien, PJ. 1935. *Will Rogers: Ambassaor of Good Will, Prince of Wit and Wisdom*. Philadelphia: John C Winston Company.

Ohio State University Archives, *Papers of Admiral Richard E. Byrd*, RG 56.1, 7739-10.

O'Neill, P. 2003. *The Oldest City: The Story of St. John's, Newfoundland*. Portugal Cove-St. Philip's, *Newfoundland and Labrador: Boulder Publications*.

Post, Wiley. *National Aviation Hall of Fame*. <http://www.nationalaviation.org>.

R-34's Historic Round Trip. Gasbags. <http://www.airship.cwc.net/R34.htm>.

Record of Service of Wing Commander Charles Sandford Wynne-Eyton, DSO 186.

Rowe, P. 1977. *The Great Atlantic Air Race*. Toronto: McClelland and Stewart.

Royal Canadian Mounted Police Annual Reports. 1927 – 1929. Ottawa: National
    Archives of Canada.

Sikorsky, II. 1938. *The Story of the Winged-S*. New York: Dodd, Mead & Company.

Sinnott, S. *Street Names of Gander*. <http://www.k12.nf.ca/sptech/projects/Grassroots/
Street-SephS/streetnames.htm>.

Smyth, R. 1997. *TheLindbergh of Canada: The Erroll Boyd Story*. Burnstown, Ontario: General
    Store Publishing House.

Them Days. September 1986.

Thomas, L. 1925. *The First World Flight*. New York: Houghton Mifflin Company.

Time. Volume 36, Number 1, 1927.

Toronto Daily Star. September 1927, April and June 1928, October 1929, August
    1930, and July 1932.

Vance, JF. 2002. *High Flight: Aviation and the Canadian Imagination*. Toronto: Penguin.

Ware, S. 1993. *Still Missing: Amelia Earhart and the Search for Modern Feminism*. New York: W.W.
    Norton and Company.

We Saw Him Land. Smithsonian. (May 2002): pp. 96-99.

Whitman, A. 1974. *Charles Lindbergh: An American Aviator*. <http://www.charleslindbergh.
    com/ny/100.asp>.

Wykes, A. 1967. *Air Atlantic: A History of Civil and Military Trans-Atlantic Flying*. London:
Hamish Hamilton.

Zanetti, G. *Francesco de Pinedo in Canada – 1927*. <http://www.giorgiozanetti.ca/pinedo/de
    pinedo.html>.

INDEX